Anonymous Heroes
D-Day June 1944
Second Edition 2019

John D. Timmins
PGC Cert. Ed.

Author's Introduction 2019.

In 2013, a DNA test confirmed who my father was. I had received his Canadian military service and casualty records, referred to as his M.F.M.4, from Veteran Affairs in Canada and I wanted to know more.

Having an enquiring mind as to what he did during WWII, from the time that he volunteered and enlisted to serve both King and Country in March 1941 until demobbed in July 1945 when he returned to his native Canada.

During my research I was to discover he surreptitiously became one of the original members of a special band of brothers that was an integral part and paramount to the success of Operation Overlord. During this research I also discovered how and why events took place leading up to D-Day.

This encouraged me to record that history exactly as it happened without any spin nor hype so that it cannot be forgotten, nor left un-told.

A quotation from a mentor of mine when I was a schoolboy prompted me to narrate this history now.

'A nation that forgets its past has no future'.

Sir Winston Leonard Spencer-Churchill,
KG, OM, CH, TD, PC, DL, FRS, RA.
(30 November 1874 – 24 January 1965)

Office of Director RCEME
National Defence Headquarters
Ottawa ON K1A 0K2
CANADA

2184-1180-1 (SO RCEME)

5 November 2015

John D. Timmins

Milton Keynes, Buckinghamshire

United Kingdom

Dear John

I would like to express my sincere gratitude to you for sharing with us your book "Anonymous Heroes". The Corps is honoured by your contribution and we appreciate you taking the time to conduct research and narrate an outstanding story that allows us to understand and appreciate RCEME contributions made in World War II.

The book you have written provides a great reminder of our proud history and heritage to all members of the Corps be they serving, retired, friends or families. As a token of our appreciation, the RCEME Corps would like to give you with a copy of the book "Afghanistan: A Canadian Story". Similar to yours, this book intends to educate and remind us of the role Canadians played in that conflict.

Again, on behalf of the Corps of RCEME, I would like to thank you for sharing your work with us.

Sincerely,

K.J. Hamilton
Colonel
Director RCEME

The Chapters

Chapter 1   Go West young man.

Alexander Alexson, my grandfather, was born in 1889 at a place called Isakivtsi in the south of what is now the independent state of Ukraine. At that time Ukraine was divided - the south from 1654 had been part of the Russian Empire and from 1849 the west lay within the Austro-Hungarian Empire.

The start of the Russian revolution of 1905 created social unrest and uncertainty throughout Russia, including Ukraine. The idea of emigration, to the New World and other parts of Europe, became popular among the working class. By this time Canada had embarked on a programme designed to increase immigration to the country's agricultural belt in the west - from Britain as the seat of the British Empire, European countries and even from the United States.

The Canadians were in particular looking to attract people from those parts of the world that showed they could be suited to the agricultural life of the Canadian prairies – including the areas that were to become the provinces of Alberta and Saskatchewan.

-By 1885, travel and communication in Canada were boosted by the completion of the Canadian Pacific Railway running from coast to coast. It was not however until 1896 that any large-scale immigration to the Canadian prairies got underway, with the railway bringing in settlers.

Between 1897 and 1911, two million people came to Canada. However, immigration would gradually become more selective over the coming years, focusing on specific skills immigrants brought to Canada. Settlers could claim up to 160 acres of free land in Canada, although they still had to pay a land registration fee. So land was not totally given away.

By 1905, with enough people living in the Northwest Territories, the Canadian federal government decided to create two new provinces, Alberta and Saskatchewan.

Readers may be unaware that the province of Saskatchewan does not have any natural borders such as rivers or mountain ranges. In fact its borders largely follow the geographic coordinates of lines of longitude and latitude making the province quadrilateral in shape with four straight sides.

Despite the harsh frontier life, the distance between communities and the arduous labour, Saskatchewan developed a thriving farming-based society in the early 1900s. The west was settled and this native prairie converted to cropland within a period of thirty years or so. Wheat became the staple crop on which the prairie economy was built, although crops such as oats, barley, and flax were also produced. Oats were mainly grown as animal feed. Farming and farm machinery were the main providers of employment in this province during that period of the early 1900s.

Members of the Alexson family recall that my grandfather arrived in Canada between 1909 -1910. However it is not until 1916 that Alexander Alexsons details are first recorded in the Canadian census of that year, stating that he settled in Saskatchewan at a place called Hazel Dell, not so far from the provincial capital city of Regina.

Parl. Bldg. at Regina, Sask.

Wedding photo, in about 1914 I'm told, my Grandfather married Maria (Mary) Koobu, my grandmother.

(Left to Right). Alexander Alexson, grandfather and Maria Koobu grandmother with brothers Fred and Thomas Alexson.

My grandmother Maria (Mary) Koobu, was an immigrant to Canada, born in 1889 in Makowisko a village in what was then the Austrian/Hungarian Empire now part of south-eastern Poland. She first went to live in Yorktown in Saskatchewan and worked in the hospital. When she married my grandfather they lived in Hazel Dell and had three children - John, Annie and my father Stephen. The family grew up in the Hazel Dell area. When the world wide flu pandemic of 1918 known as Spanish flu reached Hazel Dell in November that year it claimed my grandfather who is buried in Hazel Dell Cemetery.

As far as I know the family remained in the area. However later in the 1930s severe drought brought disaster to agriculture and farming life; both came to a virtual standstill in this region of Canada. The Great Depression set in and it was not until the end of the 1930s that the rains returned to the prairies coinciding with the outbreak of the Second World War. Both events helped bring some economic recovery to the area.

On 10 September 1939 Canada declared war on Germany sending one army division to Europe, although it had no chance of combat, before the fall of France. In 1940 Prime Minister of Canada William Mackenzie King, pledged to limit direct military involvement in the war.

Nevertheless with the outbreak of WWII the Canadian government introduced the **National Resources Mobilization Act 1940**, and one provision of this act immediately affected every adult Canadian citizen.

Citizens, both male and female, who had reached the age of 16 years, British subjects and aliens alike, were required to register at specially designated registration sites, giving the following information:-

Full name and permanent Canadian postal address. Age (last birthday) and date of birth & marital status. Number of dependants solely supported by the registrant. Country of birth, parent's country of birth, nationality, year of immigration to Canada and year of naturalization, languages spoken. Details of education, health, and general physical condition. Details of current occupation or business, including the number of years in that occupation. Details of any previous farming experience. Details of any previous military service.

A Deputy Registrar interviewed all who attended for registration, recording their details. Each citizen then signed and dated forms in the presence of the Registrar or Deputy Registrar accordingly. Basic registration details were then recorded on a card and issued similar to identity cards. Citizens were then legally obliged to carry and produce the card to any enquiring authorities and whenever requested to do so.

This registration was to identify people and any resources they may have, that could be beneficial to His Majesty King George VI for the duration of the war.

World War II officially began on 1 September 1939, with the German invasion of Poland. Britain and France had declared war on Nazi Germany on the 3 September 1939. It was just seven days later, on 10 September that the Parliament of Canada also declared war on Nazi Germany, the first time that an independent declaration of war was made by Canada.

During the Depression of the 1930s, drought turned much of Alberta and Saskatchewan, on Canada's western prairies, into a dust bowl. The rains returned to the prairies coinciding with the outbreak of the Second World War. The social and economic shock of the Great Depression had left millions of Canadians unemployed, hungry and often homeless.

The rains eventually returned but it was the onset of war that boosted employment and actually assisted the economic recovery of the area.

Chapter 2   One volunteer.

By careful scrutiny of my father's attestation papers that he completed by signing and then recording his fingerprints on the 20 of August 1941 when he took the oath of allegiance to King and Country and enlisted to serve, I have been able to learn so much about that man I never knew nor had the privilege to meet. Ironically there is a bit of déjà vu, for us both. My father was born on 21 April 1919, six months after the death of his father my grandfather. So like myself, who never got to know nor meet him, he never got to know his father, my grandfather.

One year after the death of my grandfather Alexander Alexson, my grandmother Maria (Mary) Koobu, re-married to John Chodak and then moved to a farm some three miles south of the village of Margo in Saskatchewan. This was together with her three existing children: Anne born 1915, John born 1917 and my father Steven born in April 1919. During the course of Mary's second marriage to John Chodak she had a further three children - two boys and a girl, Peter, Mike and then Mary. Mike Chodak's son Tim, a first cousin passed on these facts about my father's early life growing up in Saskatchewan.

Once again the Canadian Army (Reserve Formations) enrolment papers for volunteers, that he completed in March 1941 answer so many questions and relate to what I know about his background today.

Q7.   Religious Denomination. Roman Catholic.
Q11.   Mother Tongue.   Ukraine.
Q12.   What other Languages do you: (a) Speak?   English (b) Read?   English (c) Write? English.

Incidentally in September 2014 for the first time in our lives I met my first cousin Sylvia, the second child of my father's older sister, my aunt Anne. Sylvia confirmed as I had suspected that our grandmother did not speak English, at home only their mother tongue Ukrainian. Sylvia confirmed she was unable to communicate with our grandmother. So yes my father was bilingual.

According to these records, after leaving school for the next six years Steven worked on as a farm-helper and mechanic in Saskatchewan. On leaving school he took a job brush cutting to the west of Margo. After some months he moved over to Quill Lake, to his Uncle Fred's farm where he stayed for a number of years, before moving on to seek work in Toronto and to meet up with his older brother John who had already moved there.

Again I reflect back to the fact that on September 10 1939 Canada declared war against Germany and sent one army division (10,000 – 15,000 men) to Europe, though it had no chance for combat, before the fall of France. In 1940 Prime Minister of Canada, Mackenzie King, pledged to limit direct military involvement in the war.

Though Canada was the oldest Dominion in the British Empire, it was, for the most part, reluctant to enter the war. Canada, with a population somewhere between 11 to 12 million, eventually raised very substantial armed forces. Around 10% of the entire population of Canada joined the army, a very small amount of which was conscripted. After the long struggle of the Great Depression of the 1930s, the challenges of the Second World War accelerated Canada's ongoing transformation into a modern urban and industrialized nation.   Now information from Steven's enrolment forms, March 1941: Present address. 16 Palmerstone Ave. Toronto, Ontario, Canada. Next of Kin: Mary Chodak Relationship: Mother address: Margo, Saskatchewan.

This does confirm that by March 1941 Steven had left the wilderness prairies of Saskatchewan and moved to Ontario, another of the ten Canadian provinces, situated in what is referred to now as East-Central Canada. Ontario is bordered by the province of Manitoba to the west, Hudson Bay and James Bay to the north, and Quebec on the east, with the United States of America making up the southern boundary.

Researching the history for the town of Margo, I was able to glean from a pictorial website some old photos etc. One sentence from this website is worth quoting, to put the town's location in perspective: "In 1905 the railway reached Margo and continued west, contributing to the development of the town. The pioneers developed the town from brush land to cafes, hotels, implement dealers, livery barns and grain elevators. Margo even had

Margo in 1914

a doctor at one time".

This confirms that by 1941 it was possible to travel to Toronto by rail. So I asked my cousin Tim just how far Margo is away from Toronto; his response gives those readers who are unaware, just some idea how vast a country Canada is: - "Yes you could ride the train from Margo to Toronto in the 1940s, it probably takes about 36 hours to drive from here to Toronto". This suggests to me that my father left Saskatchewan no later than September 1940, when he moved on to Toronto seeking employment and to meet up with his older brother my uncle John.

More information taken from Steven's enrolment forms of 26 March 1941.
Q 15. Trade or Occupation...... Mechanic...... Technical Qualifications...... None.
Q 16. Previous Military Service...... None.
Q 19. Can Drive a Car.... Yes....... Repair a Motor..... Yes.......

Another important fact I have learnt from my father's attestation papers is that: Immediate Pre-Enlistment Employment: English Town Cutlery Company Toronto, employed for six months as a Mechanic.
On 20 March 1941 Steven Alexson volunteered, was accepted and sent to 23 Canadian Army (Basic) Training Centre at Newmarket, Ontario Canada.

Chapter 3   Royal Canadian Ordnance Corps.

From April to August 1941 Steven served as a reservist at the 23 Cdn. Army (Basic) Training Centre Newmarket Ontario. Due to the Great Depression and lack of an extensive apprenticeship program it was difficult to find the required tradesmen such as welders, blacksmiths, fitters, etc. During that time he attended a two-month Vehicle Mechanic's Trade classifications fitters' course on completion qualified Vehicle fitter (group C).

Classifications were group A: Fixes all things with tracks (and wheels). B. Fixes all things with wheels. C: Fixes all Plant Equipment including Generators.

During the Second World War the Royal Canadian Ordnance Corps increased from 300 of all ranks, to more than 35,000. Thousands of civilians also played their part with the Corps in Canada and overseas. The Corps was represented in every Canadian formation overseas, in all theatre of war where Canadian troops fought - France including in Dieppe, Hong Kong, Sicily, Italy and ultimately North West Europe, from Normandy where they landed with the assault forces in June 1944.

In September 1939 when war was declared the British Expeditionary Force was sent to France in support of both Belgium, and France in case Germany also invaded the Low Countries after the invasion of Poland. Nothing happened until May 1940 when Germany did invade Holland Belgium and Luxembourg and forced the British Expeditionary Force including French and Belgium forces back to the French port of Dunkirk.

I take this opportunity to remind readers by the summer of 1940 due to the aftermath of Dunkirk, Canada had to become a prime supplier of munitions. Canadian industry had to equip not only her own expanding army but also the allies as well. The Dunkirk evacuation, code-named Operation Dynamo took place between 27 May and 4 June 1940.

British Prime Minister Winston Churchill in his speech to the House of Commons he called those events in France "a colossal military disaster", saying that "the whole root and core and brain of the British Army" had been stranded at Dunkirk and seemed about to perish or be captured.

He hailed their rescue as a "miracle of deliverance". He also reminded the country: "We must be very careful not to assign this deliverance the attributes of a victory. Wars are not won by evacuations.

British Vice Admiral Ramsay, hastily assembled a fleet of over 800 boats and ships and rescued a total of three hundred and thirty-eight thousand, two hundred and twenty-six troops and evacuated them back to Britain. A miracle of deliverance.

However The British Expeditionary Force (BEF) lost 68,000 soldiers during that campaign, along with 2,472 artillery guns, 20,000 motorcycles and almost 65,000 other vehicles. All the 445 British tanks sent to France with the BEF were also abandoned. By the 22nd June 1940 the surrender of France the British had lost 1000 aircraft that had been sent to defend France. Of the 261 Hawker Hurricane fighter aircraft sent, only 66 returned with a total of 43 RAF pilots killed or lost in action, together with numerous ground crew also lost killed or captured defending British airfields in France prior to the capitulation of France.

So in 1941 the Royal Canadian Ordnance Corps was granted combatant status, and later in 1944 its Engineer branch would form the nucleus of the new Corps of Royal Canadian Electrical and Mechanical Engineers.

When the Canadian Army was looking for a European base, the British Army offered them Bordon and Longmoor camps, in Hampshire England.

Map of Bordon Military Camps Hampshire during WW II. The Canadians also constructed two new sub-camps on this site, using prefabricated wooden huts that had been built and then shipped over from Canada. Upper Oakhanger Camp, and Lower Oakhanger Camp, both occupied by Canadians. In 1942 some large sheds were also constructed on this site. The inscription on the north-east corner of one of these buildings records this event: "This corner stone was laid by Gen A C L McNaughton CB CMG DSO MC GOC-in-C 1st Canadian Army. Built for the Royal Canadian Ordnance Corps by Royal Canadian Engineers. MCMXLII." occupying these buildings was **1ˢᵗ. Canadian Base Workshop**...

Canada took over the camp entirely from September 1939. Both camps have a long association with the Canadian Army, providing a base for them in both world wars.

The British 3rd Infantry Brigade (1st Canadian Division) was resident at Bordon in 1939, but was then dispatched in its entirety at the start of hostilities of World War II, as part of the British Expeditionary Force.

The men left from Liss railway station on specially chartered trains, direct to Southampton Docks, only to be evacuated from St Malo port in Normandy France on 17 and 18 June, and returned to Portsmouth, Hampshire, England.

My father's Canadian military service and casualty records now referred to as his M.F.M.4. Records, state that on the 5 October 1941 he embarked from Halifax, Nova Scotia for England. That crossing then took twelve days.

He disembarked at Liverpool Docks Merseyside England on 17 October 1941. Canadian troops who disembarked at Glasgow Docks in Scotland or Liverpool Docks would then be transported direct by train, to Bordon campn Hampshire by military trains that ran direct into the camp.

M.F.M.4. Record states that two days after arriving in England on the 19 October 1941 my father was employed as a motor vehicle fitter grade C, based at 1st. Canadian Base Workshop located at Bordon camp Hampshire.

This workshop was destined to become the largest military workshop in the British Empire. No task was too small or too large for its personnel to undertake, from sharpening hypodermic needles for the medical corps, to the repair or rebuild of any vehicle or any other equipment, from watches to tanks. Military records show that by 1943 over 2200 personnel were employed at 1st. Canadian Base Workshop Bordon camp Hampshire.

The 1st Canadian Hussars Regiment was re-designated 6th. Armoured Regiment (1st Hussars) on 11 February 1941 and became the second senior armoured regiment of 1st Armoured Brigade, 5th Canadian Armoured Division. It embarked for the United Kingdom on 13 November 1941.

As a result of the re-organization of Canadian armoured formations, the Regiment became the senior regiment of 2nd Canadian Armoured Brigade and was also then based at Bordon camp, Hampshire.

August 1942 Carnage at Dieppe:

This was a total disaster.

The ill-fated Dieppe raid, known as the Battle of Dieppe, was an attack on the German-occupied port of Dieppe on the northern coast of France in August 1942. The raid was a total fiasco and proved that the Allies could not hope to invade mainland Europe for a long time yet to come in the war.

The assault began at 05:00 hrs. By 10:50 hrs, some five hours later, the retreat was called. Over 6,000 infantrymen, predominantly Canadian took part, supported by a Canadian Armoured regiment provided by the 14th Army Tank Regiment (The Calgary Regiment) equipped with 58 of the new Churchill tanks. Three of these were equipped with flame-thrower equipment, and all tanks were adapted to operate in the shallow water near the Dieppe beach. Unfortunately they arrived at the beach late, resulting in the two infantry battalions attacking without armoured support. When they did arrive only 29 tanks were landed. Two of the tanks sank in deep water, and 12 more became bogged down in the soft shingle beach. Only 15 tanks made it across the seawall. Once they had crossed the seawall, they were confronted by a series of tank obstacles that prevented their entry into the town. None of the tanks that did land managed to return to England.

Fire support was grossly inadequate and the raiding force was largely trapped on the beach by obstacles and German fire. All the tank crews that landed were either killed or captured. Of the 6,086 men who made it ashore 3,623 or almost 60%, were either killed, wounded, or captured. The Royal Air Force lost 96 aircraft (at least 32 to flak or accidents) and the Royal Navy lost 33 landing craft and one destroyer. Events at Dieppe gave the military planners much to contemplate and certainly influenced preparations for Operation Torch in 1942 and Operation Overlord in June 1944.

The pages of history record when man started to wage tactical warfare, not just 'hit and run raids' but planned battles using tactics and strategy. From Roman times to our twentieth century wars, most armies have been accompanied by craftsmen weapons makers, for example: the Fletcher, a craftsman who made arrows.

The Bowyer a craftsman who made bows; the Blacksmith and Ironworker craftsmen who made Armour. The Farrier was a specialist in equine hoof care, which included making horse shoes, the Wheelwright a craftsman who built or repaired wheels, right up to our modern day motor mechanic and vehicle fitter.

All of these craftsmen supported and assisted armies as they were prepared and departed for war. They travelled with the main body of the army but were mostly detached from the main assault troops when in battle, although they would give support as and when required, repairing or replacing damaged equipment. With the development of mechanisation and modern warfare, detachments of these specialist craftsman evolved to assist and give support to all battle groups. I'm reliably informed that the terminology of Light Aid Detachment originated during WW1 1914 -1918, when the Royal Ordnance Corp craftsman armourers worked out of the backs of lorries that had been placed near to artillery gun batteries, the lorries being used as small mobile repair shops. Any artillery pieces needing repair or replacement could be worked on immediately, minimising the time that an artillery piece was out of action and away from gun batteries.

The following explanation is taken direct from the British Army's own website about Light Aid Detachments. Each regiment will have Royal Electrical and Mechanical Engineers [REME] soldiers attached to it. The soldiers normally form a small workshop that is called a Light Aid Detachment **LAD.** From here, REME soldiers can maintain and repair the units equipment where and when it breaks down.

If the repair is too large and complex they can ask the REME battalion to carry out the repairs. In the battlefield, the LAD will follow the unit, therefore the LAD will also drive and operate similar vehicles to the unit that they are in support of.

Illustration of a 1940's Chevrolet 2 Ton 4 x 4 Light Recovery Truck.

(M.F.M.4) records: On 14 June 1942, after some seven months, my father was transferred from the Base Workshop to '54 LAD' in support of 6th. Armoured Regiment (1st Hussars) of the 5th Canadian Armoured Division as a Motor Vehicle Fitter group C. His detachment would be a part of the main unit to enable them when needed to undertake certain repairs as first line on the spot. This included the light aid detachments, which could deploy quickly to recover or repair equipment on the battlefield, or even in transit to the front line. Some elements of light aid detachments would move out on manoeuvres and accompany the main force, as this was a good experience for training away from the main workshop. All personnel were RCOC qualified and skilled tradesmen, having gained expertise with the maintenance of armoured fighting vehicles and the other equipment that this unit would be using.

Research shows that the typical composition of a LAD was around 60-80 personnel, just a small detachment of craftsmen attached to a host battalion to support and maintain the battalion's equipment. Again the actual size was very much dependent on the host battalion's equipment that the LAD was required to support and maintain.

Normally the LAD would have their own commanding officer, usually holding the rank of captain and in overall charge of the LAD but also supported by a Warrant Officer (WO) This rank was introduced into the British Army in 1879 and is the highest group of non-commissioned ranks, holding the King's (or Queen's warrant), which is signed by the Secretary of State for Defence. Currently there are only two classes of Warrant Officer Ranks.

Warrant Officer First Class.

Warrant Officer Second Class.

The LAD would then be split up into two groups, one of about 30 men who would make up a mobile workshop to handle any larger repairs that could not be carried out on the front line of the battlefield. The remaining group of the detachment personnel would make up fitter sections, each of about 5 - 7 men, which would accompany the main battle group or squadron into battle. The aim was to remain just a short distance behind the main assault group, so they could be called forward when safe to carry out any repairs or retrieve equipment. This could then be taken back to the mobile workshop if a major repair or rebuild was required, the aim being to get defective equipment back into action as rapidly as possible.

Armoured recovery vehicle

Equipment sometimes would break down on its way to the battlefield, which meant prompt recovery and repair to maintain the strength of that fighting unit. This was an average configuration of numbers for a LAD and does of course vary widely, being dependent on the parent unit and the equipment that they would be using to fulfil its role in the battle plan or military objective.

As the name suggests, the 1st Hussars Canada is a cavalry regiment. The regimental history shows that its roots can be traced back to its formation in March 1856 as a volunteer cavalry militia. Over the years members of the Hussars have distinguished themselves in most theatres of war, from the second Boer War in South Africa in October 1899, to the outbreak of the First World War in 1914 when members joined the Canadian Expeditionary Force and participated at the second battle of Ypres, the battle of Flers-Courcelette, battle of Hill 70 and the battle of Passchendaele.

At the start of the First World War the British army's hierarchy was dominated by officers from cavalry regiments, and at first the engagements between British and German troops did involve cavalry. However, trench warfare nullified the use of cavalry, since cavalry engagements in mud proved very costly and, from a military standpoint, hopeless.

The idea of the tank came about with the development of farming vehicles that had the ability to cross difficult land surfaces and overcome challenging conditions such as deep mud, large holes and wide ditches, these conditions made easier by vehicles driven on caterpillar tracks.

Britain and France developed tanks to overcome barbed wire and other obstacles in no-man's land as well as to give protection from machine-gun fire. British tanks first went into action on the Somme in 1916.

Royal Tank Corps Cap Badge WWII

The Germans produced few tanks and then not until late in WWI, a total of 20, compared to nearly 4,000 French and over 2,500 British tanks. It was during WWI that the first tank-versus-tank battle took place in April 1918. After WWI armored warfare became more sophisticated and saw the birth of specialist armored regiments. By WWII Germany had learned the importance of tanks and had developed the strategy of Blitzkrieg, or 'lightning war'. This involved the use of dense concentrations of tanks in support of mechanized infantry formations, supported by the German Luftwaffe's (air force) dive-bombers which attacked enemy positions just before a tank assault.

By the second year of WWII in 1940, the German Wehrmacht (army) had overrun or walked through Denmark, Norway, Belgium, the Netherlands, and Luxembourg and into France using 'Blitzkrieg' tactics. This is why the British Expeditionary Force (BEF) and its allies was devastatingly pushed back and forced to retreat, with the Forces being evacuated from Dunkirk in June 1940.

The 1st Hussars became part of Canada's Armored Corps when it was raised in August 1940. The Corps trained using various makes of Light Tanks developed during the 1930s. Although obsolete, these tanks served the purpose of training the regiment in tactics and vehicle maintenance. In October 1941 the 1st Hussars (now the 6th Armoured Regiment) became part of the 1st Canadian Armored Brigade, sent to England in October 1941. On arrival in the United Kingdom they took up residence in Aldershot and continued training.

Aldershot in Hampshire is the home of the British Army and was the first military camp when built in 1854, during the reign of Queen Victoria. Aldershot is just 35 miles southwest of London and close to the seaports of Portsmouth and Southampton, making it an ideal military base. Bordon and Longmoor military camps, where my father Steve was based when part of 1st. Canadian Base Workshop, after arriving in England about the same time as the 1st Hussars in October 1941. Tank and armored regiment do different jobs during battles, using the different classes of tanks: light, medium or heavy tanks.

Tank design had gradually improved after WWI, reflecting the growth of the automotive industry, as tank engines, transmissions, and track systems greatly improved. By the beginning of WWII in September 1939, tanks could travel hundreds of miles on their tracks, however heavily dependent on petrol, oil and other lubricants, and the right technical support.

Infantry Tanks were heavily armored, good for most types of terrain but very slow. At first, speed, was never considered an advantage in tanks, as they were designed to support infantry assaults on enemy strong points. Cruiser Tanks were intended for independent maneuvering, reconnaissance, and flanking attacks. The early Cruiser Tanks gained performance only at a cost of reducing the thickness of the armor, thereby reducing weight to gain extra speed.

Late in 1943 the 1st Hussars Canada were issued with the M4 Sherman tank, officially classed as a Medium Tank. The M4 was the second most produced tank during World War II it was named after the American Civil War General, William Tecumseh Sherman.

Its relative ease of production contributed to the huge numbers of M4 Sherman tanks produced, in fact some 49,234 where manufactured during the period 1941 to 1945. This availability played a major part with tank recovery. Repair units could cannibalize parts from heavily disabled vehicles, then repair and return others less damaged back in to service ready for action again. Repairing on the spot was far quicker than towing them away and waiting for spare parts to become available.

The M4 Sherman's weighed approximately 30 tons.

Its armour was approximately 3" inches thick a maximum of 76 millimeters. The main armament was one 75 millimeter gun, for which the tank could carry 90 rounds of ammunition. The secondary armament was one .50 caliber Browning Machine gun with 300 rounds of ammunition. Other armaments in support where two 30 caliber Browning Machine guns and approximately 5000 rounds of ammunition. The top speed depended on ground conditions and the terrain but an average speed of approximately 25 to 30 mph was advised.

In May 1942 the basic organization settled at 55 standard cruiser tanks in one Armored Regiments. The M4 used a crew of five: commander, gunner, loader, driver and co-driver.

Chapter 6

54 LAD, R.C.O.C with 5th Canadian Armoured Division.

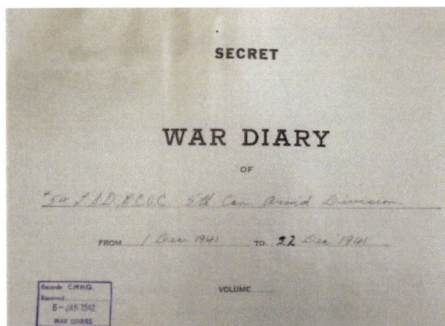

War Office records referenced WO 166/1363619 held at the British National Archives, records from day one some details about the establishment and development of 54 LAD. I was surprised, when opening the file, to discover some handwritten notes and a hand drawn diagram similar to this now:

The details in this chart suggests that this was the birth of 54 LAD, and this was the composition of the detachment at its initial concept when established in September 1941.

From reading the typed up reports that followed those hand written notes, I learned that this detachment actually arrived in Aldershot on Saturday 1st November 1941 when allocated to accommodation at Waterloo Barracks.

L.A.D. Type C. W.E. Personnel as of 21/9/41

Detail	Officers	W.O's	S. SGTS, & SGTS	Rank & File	Total
Captain O.M.E.	1				1
ARMAMENT. ART.		1 (WOII)	3 (a)		4
ARTISANS				9	9 (6)
CLERKS				1	1
STORE MEN				2 (c)	2
Non Tradesmen				3	3
TOTAL LAD	1	1	3	15	20

Establishment of other Ranks By Trade & DUTIES.

ARMAMENT ARTIFICER A.F.V.	4
ARTISANS - DRIVER - MECHANICS	3
ELECTRICIANS (d)	1
FITTERS (e)	4
WELDERS (e)	1
CLERKS	1
STOREMEN	2
TRADESMEN TOTAL	16

BATMAN DRIVER	1
DRIVERS I.C.	1
MOTORCYCLISTS	1
NONE-TRADESMEN Total	3

The report then states that the detachment was granted four days leave referred to as 'Landing Leave' which suggests they had recently arrived in the UK from Canada. After ten to twelve days on a troopship, crossing the North Atlantic Ocean during winter from a different time zone, I can understand [22] need for a few days to acclimatise to new surroundings especially considering that during the war years Great Britain had substantially adjusted time keeping to maximise daylight working hours. From 1940, clocks in Britain were not just put back by one hour at the end of Summer Time.

In subsequent years, clocks continued to be advanced by one hour each spring and put back by an hour each autumn until July 1945. During these summers, therefore, Britain was two hours ahead of GMT and working on British Double Summer Time (BDST). So the need to give these Canadian craftsmen 'Landing Leave' time to adjust and acclimatise to their new surroundings can be understood as well as to give time for stores and equipment to arrive and be allocated to the new unit.

In that file I found copies of training programmes and other notes, and was interested to read that some trade qualifications held by some of these tradesmen gained in Canada had to be re-studied and then re-taken in England because the British Army did not recognised them. So for most of November 1941 some members of the detachments spent time in the classroom bringing qualifications up to scratch.

An entry from the 17th November indicates that their allocation of hand tools had arrived finally at Didcot Military Barracks.

[During WWII Didcot's railway junction gave rail access routes to London, Bristol, Oxford and on to Southampton via the Didcot, Newbury and Southampton Railway (DN&S). This made Didcot of strategic importance to military logistics, especially during the Second World War.]

Again this does suggest that this detachment was a complete new unit being fitted out as part of some long term master military plan. Over the next few weeks according to the carbon copies of training schedules in file WO 166/1363619, one week was spent by all members of the unit on weapons training, at different firing ranges. These range sessions applied only to three types of weapons, the .303 calibre Bren gun, 7.92mm calibre Besa Machine Gun, and the .45 calibre Thompson submachine gun.

Despite having some knowledge of British military weapons I was not familiar with the   **7.92mm calibre Besa Machine Gun.**

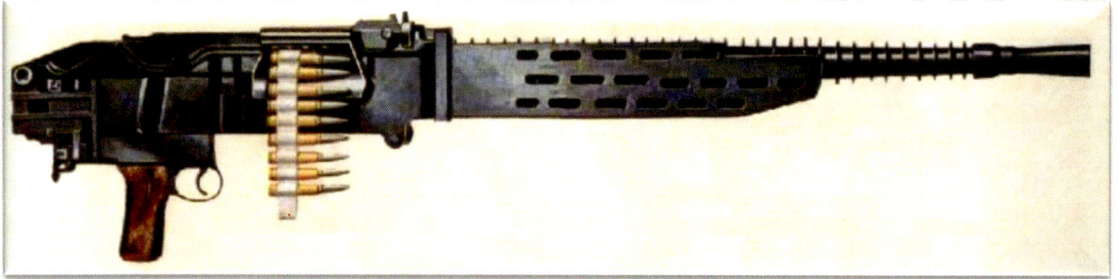

I discovered that it was a belt-fed machinegun used extensively by the British armed forces during the Second World War as a mounted machine gun on tanks and other armoured vehicles, being introduced to replace a much heavier, water-cooled machine gun. Machineguns that require water to cool the barrel had limited usage in some theatres of war, such as deserts or in arctic conditions where water was not readily available. Air cooling systems provided more versatility, and having a belt-fed ammunition systems minimises the weight of ammunition on the loading mechanism, which both allowed a high rate of continuous fire and reduced stoppages. The name Besa came from the British manufacturer the Birmingham Small Arms Company. The calibre of ammunition used 7.92 mm the same size as that used by the German Wehrmacht. In fact the 7.92 Mauser cartridge was one of the world's most popular military cartridges in both world wars.

Although fitted with a bipod, the Bren gun could also be mounted on a tripod or vehicle-mounted. One of the manufacturer was John Inglis and Company based in Toronto Canada.

In March 1938 the company won a contract with the British and Canadian governments to supply 5,000 Bren machine guns to Great Britain and 7,000 to Canada. This versatile light machine gun was to remain in service with the British Army well into the 1990s. As seen in this illustration .303 ammunition is held in the curved magazine that could hold 30 rounds, although in practice usually only 27 or 28 rounds, to prevent jams and avoid wearing out the magazine spring that fed the ammunition into the firing mechanism. The Bren was a gas-operated weapon and its .303 ammunition was the same as the standard British rifle, the Lee-Enfield. The Bren was used on many vehicles, including the Universal Carrier, which gave that vehicle the alternative name of Bren Gun Carrier, also on tanks, armoured cars and Lorries.

All members joining 54 LAD were trained to be proficient with these two particular weapons, learning about the likely causes of stoppages, obviously because these were the two weapons they would come in contact with when repairing or recovering vehicles from the battlefield.

However the Thompson submachine gun was the preferred personal weapon used by tank and other vehicle crewmen because of its compactness, the reliability of its large .45 calibre cartridge, and it's high rate of automatic fire and was widely utilised by British and Canadian units. Its stopping power, made the weapon very effective in the kinds of close combat and confined spaces that craftsmen found themselves working, particularly in the street fighting they frequently encountered during the invasion of France.

The Thompson had provision for both box and drum magazines. The drum magazines held fifty rounds of ammunition, but the British Army did not approve of the excessive weight and the rattling sound they made, an extended twenty-round box magazine was produced. In contrast, the twenty round box magazine was light and compact, and tended not to rattle. It was quickly attached and detached, and being removed downward made clearing jams easier. An empty box magazine could easily be reloaded with loose rounds. However, users complained it was limited in its capacity and in the field, users frequently taped two twenty round magazines together to speed up magazine changes.

By April 1942 a thirty round box magazine (as illustrated) had been developed.

By the end of World War II in 1945, over 1.5 million Thompson submachine guns had been produced for wartime use by Britain and her allies.

Chapter 7

Unit Identification

Canadian soldiers wore similar uniforms to the British. In 1939 at the beginning of the war some differences did exist, but these were soon ironed out. Obtaining replacement uniforms became difficult when posted overseas, because the Canadian battledress was made of a better quality cloth in a different shade of Khaki. However, badges of rank conformed to the British pattern, which meant that cap badges and collar 'dogs' were the only way of identifying Canadian units, although cloth shoulder titles and formation insignia patches stating the unit's nationality as shown in the example above were worn.

I was informed by the Technical Historian of the REME museum of technology, that the Canadian army system of giving each Light Aid Detachment its own number differed from the British system, which simply used the parent unit's title first, then the suffix '**LAD REME**'. Having spent many months researching unit 54 LAD in both British and Canadian War Office files and diaries, when I have come across any reference to the title 54 LAD, providing the dates cross reference with those recorded in my father's M.F.M.4. I know its safe to assume he was with the unit at that particular time.

The British War diary file WO 166/1363619 for November - December 1941 reveals from an entry made on 17th November that the whole unit moved to Crowbrough in Berkshire to train with the 8th Armoured division and was integrated with that division's personnel. Each craftsman was teamed up, trade by trade , driver with a driver, welders with welders and so forth. This entry also recorded that the unit attended a lecture given by a British major about his experiences of Escape and Evasion from German POW camps during WWI.

Also in December 1941, 54 LAD was attached to support another Canadian

tank regiment that had arrived in England at the end of November 1941 the Fort Garry Horse, known as the Garry's an ex-cavalry regiment that originated from Winnipeg in the province of Manitoba. This regiment had also participated with the Canadian Expeditionary Force in WWI, taking part in many actions, both as a cavalry regiment and by relieving infantry units in the trenches throughout 1916.

In notable action in **November 1917, 'B' squadron of the** Garry's, **now part** of the Canadian Cavalry Brigade, 5th Cavalry Division, was assigned as advance guard for the Division and had been given a special mission to capture a German corps headquarters. In advance of the main regiment 'B' squadron who had managed to cross the canal using a temporary bridge, leaving the remainder of the regiment held up because the main bridge over that canal had collapsed under the weight of a tank. The regimental commanding officer received orders to cancel the entire cavalry advance. Unfortunately **'B' squadron was** already on its way and did not receive that order. Despite coming under heavy machine gun fire, which killed the officer in charge, a lieutenant immediately took command and led 'B' squadron forward charging with swords drawn, against a German artillery battery, which they destroyed. From the original 129 men and 140 horses only 43 men and horses were left. **After dark, the horses were stampeded as a diversion, allowing the men to make their way back through the German lines on foot, bringing back nine prisoners. The** lieutenant **was awarded the Victoria Cross for this action.**

Not the first time in history, men on horses had charged artillery batteries, with swords drawn. On 25 October 1854 at the Battle of Balaclava during the Crimean War the British Light Brigade took a similar course of action and charged batteries of Russian artillery guns. This goes to show how little the strategies of warfare had changed over the succeeding 60 or so years.

Not too long after Britain's declaration of war on Nazi Germany in September 1939 the Fort Garry Horse were mobilized and posted to Camp Borden Ontario, where training began as an armoured regiment. Like the 1st Hussars they became part of Canada's Armoured Corps raised in August 1940. The first tanks that the Fort Garry Horse used for training were obsolete American six ton machines built in 1918. At this stage America had not entered the war, and her neutrality laws prohibited the sale of weapons to Canada. So those obsolete machines had been sold to Camp Borden's iron foundry under the guise of being scrap metal, to get round the neutrality laws. These obsolete machines served the purpose as the Garry's got them in running order, learning the basics of tank manoeuvre and tank maintenance. The first live firing exercises did not take place until July 1942 when the regiment was on manoeuvres on tank firing ranges in Wales.

In December 1942 the Garry's returned to their main base at Hove in the south of England, and together with the 1st Hussars and the Sherbrook Fusiliers, and formed the 3rd Canadian Army Tank Brigade. At the same time my father's unit 54 LAD was assigned to support and work with that tank brigade.

File WO 166/1363619 gave me my next clue in that these tank manoeuvres were all part and parcel of a master plan for the preparation of the invasion of mainland Europe.

An entry from 24 of November records: '3 Scammells' being received from 1 Rec Coy. This abbreviation 'Rec Coy' I suspect does in fact refer to 1st Recovery Company.

Scammell Lorries Limited was a British manufacturer of trucks that had specialised in military off-road vehicles from 1921. Its history went back to the late Victorian period to George Scammell himself, a wheelwright and coach-builder. Another notable family member was Lt Col Alfred Scammell, who was injured and invalided out of the army during WWI. His practical experience gained during that war, led the company to concentrate on articulated and rigid wheeled lorries mainly for the military, as well as for the heavy haulage trades. One vehicle that became well-used was the six-wheeled Pioneer, an off-road heavy haulage tractor, first produced in 1927. The Pioneer showed outstanding cross-country performance due to its design, and it formed the basis of the British Army's World War II 30-ton tank transporter. With the outbreak of war, development of new vehicles by Scammell stopped and production concentrated instead on military Pioneers for use as artillery tractors, recovery and transporter vehicles.

Illustration is of a late 1940's early 1950's six-wheeled Scammell Pioneer.

Chapter 8.

The Pivotal Years.

By December 1941 Japan had been at War with China for some four years since 1937.

On the morning of 7th December 1941 there was an unprovoked attack by Japanese naval and air forces on the American Pacific fleets, at their Pearl Harbour base on the island of Oahu Hawaii in the Pacific Ocean. Without a declaration of war or any explicit warnings. This was planned by the Japanese as a preventive action to keep the American fleets from interfering with military action that Japan was planning in Southeast Asia against the overseas territories of the United Kingdom, the Netherlands, and also the United States. The attack was a profound shock to America. On the following day 8 December, the American president Franklin D. Roosevelt, made a passionate speech to the US congress in which he called December 7, 1941 "a date which will live in infamy". He asked congress to declare war on Japan, which they did, in reaction to which both Nazi Germany and Italy declared war on the US in support of their ally Japan. So in reality it was some two years and three months after the declaration of war against Nazi Germany and her allies by Great Britain and Canada that the US officially joined WWII on the 11 December 1941.

A conference was held in Casablanca, French Morocco in January 1943 attended by the British Prime Minister Winston Churchill and United States

President Franklin D. Roosevelt together with representatives from the Free French Forces, Generals Charles de Gaulle and Henri Giraud. The leaders agreed the specifics of tactical procedure, the allocation of resources, and the broader conduct of the

war at that stage. The most important agreement reached was to the effect that the only way the war would end was by the 'unconditional surrender' of the Axis powers as Nazi Germany, Italy and Japan were now referred to.

The Russian leader Joseph Stalin did not attend that first wartime 'summit' in Casablanca because the battle of Stalingrad required his presence at home.

The Battle of Stalingrad was fought from August 1942 to February 1943. Stalingrad now called Volgograd lies in the southwest of Russia about 600 miles from Moscow. The battle was a turning point of World War II because for the first time the German Wehrmacht was decisively defeated. More to the point the battle meant the withdrawal of vast military forces from Western Europe by the Wehrmacht, to reinforce losses in Russia. At this time the Allied Forces were preparing initial plans for the invasion of Nazi held mainland Europe for later in 1943.

In May 1943 the defeat and surrender of remnants of the German Afrikakorps, along with all other remaining Axis forces in North Africa, boosted the morale of the British people and proved that Nazi Germany was not invincible. That conference also agreed that at that stage of the war, the main priority was to defeat the German Kriegsmarine U-boats, which were attacking and sinking supply ships, thus stopping a large proportion of imported materials and resources reaching the United Kingdom. This was impeding war production as well as lowering the morale of the British people through severe food rationing. Therefore the next phase after the defeat of the U-boats was to plan an invasion of mainland Europe.

The conference agreed Sicily was to be the target for invasion in 1943. Britain and her allies were no longer looking over their shoulders anticipating an attack by Nazi Germany on England. Planning and training began for the Sicily campaign as is self-evident from the secret War Diaries held in the national archives at Kew, in Surrey England.

In an entry of **War Diary** dated 22 November 1943 there is reference to unit **22 BRS REME**, being issued with three Scammell lorries and proceeding to Scotland on exercise 'Vidi-Push' with **7 Beach Group**. I was keen to know more about a 'Beach group'.

The next entry in that **War Diary** of 3 December 1943 reads: "Arrived back from exercise 'Vidi-Push", which meant they had been out on manoeuvres for a period of 10 days. From a military standpoint the location, Scotland could be very important, but more to the point resources could not have been so restricted, namely petrol, oil and lubricants, commonly referred to as P O & L. Regiments of tanks burn up petrol as do other support vehicles.

On British television (2014) I remember some veterans talked about training at that time and how in 1943, live tank firing if and when the opportunity did arise was restricted to two rounds of tank ammunition per tank per month and then only when available.

War Diary entry from the 8 December 1943, at 17.30 hrs. makes interesting reading to anyone with an enquiring military mind: Increment arrives from Holding Centre REME 2nd Lieutenant Whitley. Party comprises of AQMS Woodburn & 54 NCOs and men, making the unit strength now:
2 Officers (1 Captain and 1 Second Lieutenant)

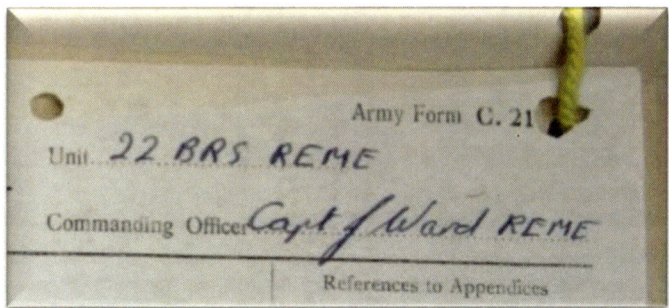

1 Warrant Officer (AQMS)
2 Staff Sergeants.   5 Sergeants.   4 Corporals 2 Lance Corporals 66 Craftsmen & privates.   (40 men without   weapons)   **Total unit strength 82.**

War Diary entry form the 12 December.   1 Sgt & 8 men with 1 Scammell proceed on exercise "Cropper II". Entry form the 22 December.   1 Ford 3 ton GS 4 x 4 lorry collected VRD. Entry form the 24 December. The unit less the rear party move to Scotland for   exercise "Roundabout II".

Entry form the 25 December 3 motor cycles collected from VRD. Away in Scotland some 600 miles from their base at Winterbourne in Hampshire in the south of England on Christmas Eve 1943 and on military exercises and manoeuvres? Surreptitiously and very covertly this unit 22 BRS REME was formed as were so many other **'Band of Brothers' in WWII.**

Chapter 9

The Atlantic Wall.

Nazi Germany invaded Denmark and occupied Norway on the same day, 9 April 1940. Neighbouring Sweden maintained her neutrality throughout the war. On 10 May 1940 the Germans also invaded Holland, Belgium and Luxemburg. Winston Churchill, the British Prime Minister, was becoming increasingly concerned the Germans would soon try to establish a military presence in Iceland. Early on the morning of 10 May 1940 Operation Fork was put into action by the Royal Navy when a small force of 746 Royal Marines entered Reykjavík harbour the capital of neutral Iceland. The Icelandic Prime Minister gave orders to his police force not to interfere with the British troops and to prevent any conflict between the Icelanders and the Royal Marines. This initial force was later replaced by a larger occupation force of 25,000 British and Canadian troops. On 7 July 1941 the defence of Iceland was transferred to the United States from British forces.

In 1941 Great Britain and her allies carried out raids on the clusters of islands just off the Norwegian coast called the Lofoten Islands. In March, Operation Claymore destroyed factories producing fish oil and glycerine, products required by the German war industry. In August, Operation Gauntlet, a combined operation by Canadian troops and free Norwegian forces, destroyed the coal mines owned by Norway, preventing their usage by the Germans.

Following Operation Chariot, the raid on St. Nazaire docks in France, in April 1942 Adolf Hitler ordered naval and submarine bases to be heavily defended. These fortifications remained concentrated around ports until late in 1943 when defences were increased in other areas. While still fighting the Russians on the eastern front, but anticipating further invasions along the Atlantic coast, Hitler gave orders to construct large coastal defences along the coastline stretching the 3,500 miles from Norway down to the Pyrenees the mountain region that is the border between France and Spain.

These defences became known as the 'Atlantic Wall'.

[Depicted on this map by this broken line]

It must have been obvious to the Axis powers that Britain and her Allies were building up for a major action - in all probability the invasion of mainland Europe.

In 1943 reports to Hitler revealed that the Atlantic Wall was more show than substance, with construction substantially behind schedule. Early in 1944 Hitler appointed Field Marshal Erwin Rommel to command 'Army Group B' because of his leadership of the German and Italian forces during the North African campaign which had established him as one of the most able and skilled commanders of the war. Never a member of the Nazi party Rommel was regarded as a humane and professional soldier and was responsible for improving the Atlantic Wall's defenses from Denmark to Brittany. Rommel firmly believed the existing coastal fortifications were entirely inadequate and immediately began to strengthen them.

To accomplish this, Rommel first improved the conditions for the Todt Organization workers. In a speech to a German Wehrmacht division based near Le Havre, at the mouth of the River Seine, he said, "Pay workers well and promptly for it. Point out that the enemy is least likely to invade where most obstacles have been erected. The French farmers will be only too glad to line their purses."

Rommel firmly believed that Nazi Germany would inevitably be defeated unless any invasion could be stopped on the beaches. Reinforced concrete pillboxes were built along the beaches as well as inland, to house machine guns, anti-tank guns and light artillery. Rommel put his own troops to work with the Todt Organization workers as well as the French labourers, who did get paid good wages for the work. Mines and anti-tank obstacles were planted on the beaches and underwater obstacles and mines were placed in waters just offshore. The plan was to destroy the Allied landing craft before they could unload troops and equipment on to the beaches.

Known as Dragons Teeth

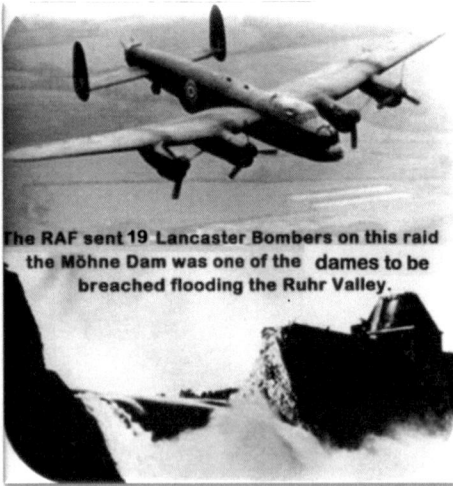

The RAF sent 19 Lancaster Bombers on this raid the Möhne Dam was one of the dames to be breached flooding the Ruhr Valley.

Operation Chastise, better known as the Dam busters Raid, was an attack in May 1943 by the RAF 617 Squadron, with the objective of destroying German dams in the Ruhr valley the industrial heartland of the German war machine. Factories in the area were heavily committed to producing aircraft, ammunition and tanks for the final assault on the Russians on the eastern front.

Two of these dams were breached and the raid that had a devastating effect on Nazi war production. In addition to providing hydro-electric power and pure water for steel-making, the dams also supplied drinking water as well as water for the canal transport system.

What was not known at the time nor appreciated was that the Todt organization workers had to immediately relocate to the Ruhr to repair this damage. The thousands working on the Atlantic Wall in the Normandy area of France were sent to Germany, together with millions of tons of materials originally designated for the fortifications in Normandy along the Atlantic Wall. The Nazi war machine was put out of action for five to six months in the Ruhr valley, and loss of production of armaments had a significant effect on the final outcome of the war. But nowhere was this more costly to the Germans than on the beaches of Normandy.

By May 1943 Great Britain was home to thousands of US airmen from the 8th Army Air Force some 100,000 of them based in East Anglia. In June strategic bombing began directly aimed at the German war production factories, the American army air force bombing by day and the RAF by night.

USAAF based in East Anglia 1943.

Chapter 10 Operations Torch & Mincemeat.

The Second Front: Disinformation : Selling Deception:

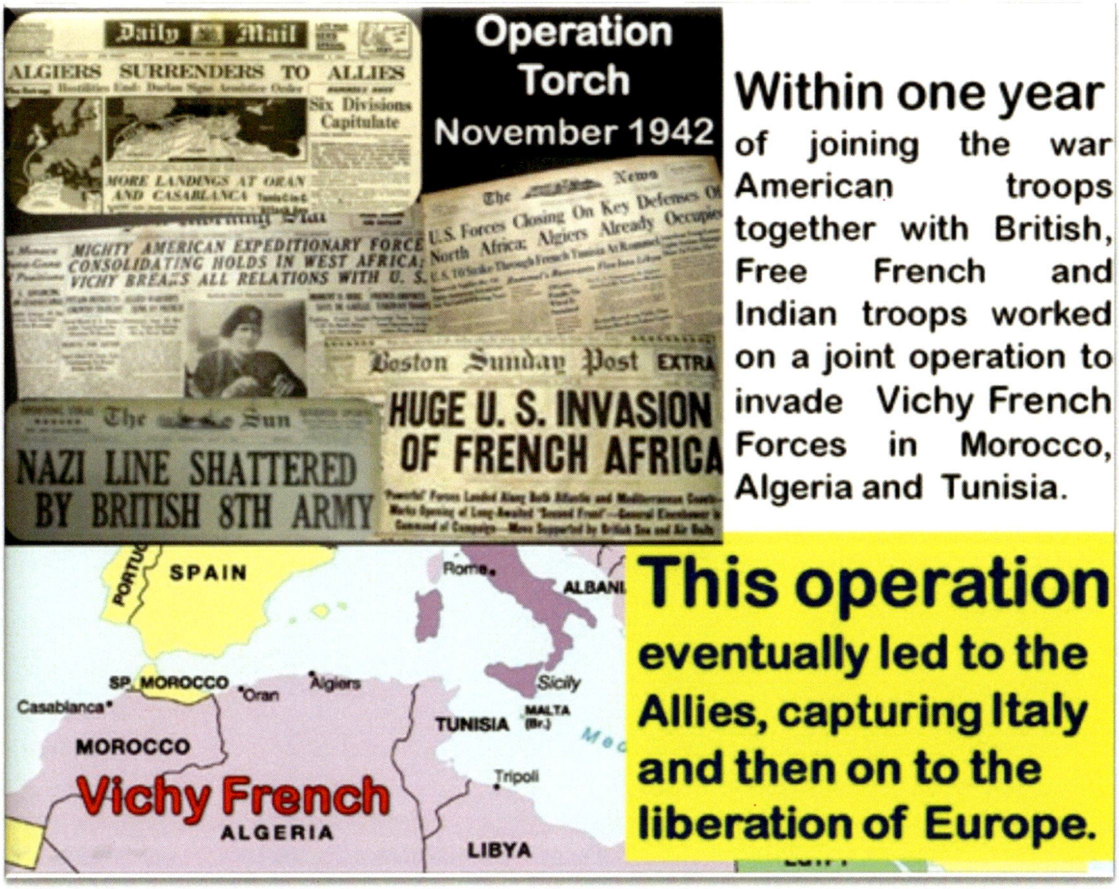

By April 1943, the war in North Africa (Morocco, Algeria and Tunisia) was almost over for the Axis powers. Allied air forces had cut off Axis supplies into North Africa and American forces landed in Morocco in November 1942 had then pushed Axis troops into Tunisia. At the same time British and commonwealth troops had driven Axis troops from Libya and into Tunisia.
The Allies now had control of the air and sea, preventing any large-scale evacuation of Axis troops from Tunisia. By 13 May, the Axis forces had surrendered and 275,000 German and Italian troops were captured. This loss of experienced troops greatly reduced the military capacity of the Axis powers in North Africa.

The first wartime 'summit' at Casablanca in January 1943, at which the Allies agreed that with Sicily as the target, the Allied invasion back into mainland Europe could go ahead. This would open up the agreed 'Second Front', forcing the Nazis to fight two major land campaigns against the Russians on the eastern front and the Allies in the southern Mediterranean area.

With North Africa controlled by the Allies and the Mediterranean open for Allied shipping, an invasion of continental Europe from North Africa was possible. Attacks could be made either into Italy or through Greece and the Balkans, trapping the Nazi forces between the Western Allies and the Russians. Looking at the map, Sicily was an obvious strategic objective and German planners would also know this. As Prime Minister Winston Churchill commented "Everyone but a bloody fool would know that it's **Sicily** next."

Churchill was concerned that the massive Allied buildup of resources in North Africa ready for an invasion would be counteracted by the Nazis bringing in more fighting units. However, if the Allies could deceive the Nazis as to the location of the attack the Nazi' might disperse or divert significant part of their forces away.

British military intelligence therefore came up with the idea of Operation Mincemeat, a plan to pass disinformation directly to the German Abwehr as to the real target area for Operation Husky the code name for an invasion in the Mediterranean area.

Operation Mincemeat was based on a real incident in September 1942. When an American PBY Catalina flying boat carrying top secret documents from England to Gibraltar, crashed in the sea off the coast of Cadiz in neutral Spain with no survivors. One body that of a VIP courier, was washed up on a Spanish beach and handed back to the British authorities in Madrid. British military intelligence was surprised that top secret letters still on this body had not been opened.

Although Spain maintained neutrality throughout WWII, in 1936 the Nazi leader, Adolf Hitler had sent powerful air and armoured units to assist the nationalist's forces led by General Franco, fighting in the Spanish Civil War from 1936 - 39. When the nationalists triumphed in 1939, Franco established an autocratic dictatorship. As a supporter of Fascism and of the Nazi party Franco would be bound to help the Germans by passing on any secret information via the German embassy in Madrid.

On the night of 30 April 1943 a man's body dressed in a Royal Marines battledress and coat, wearing the rank of a major was pushed out from HMS Seraph, a British submarine, less than a mile off the coast of Spain, near the town of Huelva a seaport in the Andalusia region.

A military courier's briefcase was attached to the wrist by a handcuff and chain. On the body was various fake documents and in the pockets, a photo of a girlfriend, a fake military identity card in the name of Major William Martin, Royal Marines, as well as a letter from his bank manager informing him that he was overdrawn.

The body also had his pass card to Combined Operations HQ. British military intelligence got the London Times of 4 June 1943 to report the death of Major Martin in a plane crash over the sea, in case the Germans came upon the body. To add to the plot, the British Admiralty sent several messages to the British Naval Attaché at the British Embassy in Madrid asking about the papers that Major Martin had been carrying and about the fake maps and letters in the briefcase.

One letter was from the Chief of Combined Operations Commodore Louis Mountbatten addressed to General Dwight D. Eisenhower Supreme Commander of the Allied Expeditionary Forces. In his purported letter, Mountbatten asked Eisenhower to write a brief foreword note for a pamphlet to be issued to all American troops about Operation Husky a plan to invade mainland Europe from Sardinia and into Greece, then up through Macedonia, there was no mention of Sicily.

On the night of 30 April on an incoming tide the body of Major William Martin, "the man who never was", slipped over the side and into the sea off Huelva a seaport in southwestern Spain.

British military intelligence knew that a German Abwehr agent was living in Huelva and friendly with the Spanish officials in the town. The body was duly, found by a local fisherman the next morning, and handed over to the Spanish police, normal practice when bodies were washed up. Identified as being British, the Vice Consul at the British embassy in Madrid was contacted, who arranged for a pathologist to perform a post-mortem examination. The pathologist reported that the man had fallen into the sea while still alive, had no bruises, that death was due to drowning, and that the body had been in the sea for three to five days. Details of Major Martin were included in the list of British casualties that normally appeared in The Times by coincidence on 4 June, when the names of two other officers who had died when their plane was lost at sea these were also published, giving credence to the Major Martin story. Soon the most senior Abwehr agent in Spain, was taking a keen interest, and before long with the assistance of Spain's secret police the contents of the briefcase were being photographed and sent to Abwehr headquarters in Germany.

Within days, Axis forces were being redirected away from the Sicily region and reinforcements sent directly to Greece, Sardinia and Corsica instead. British commando activities in Greece also helped to fool the Nazis that Greece was the main target for this invasion. Adolf Hitler sent Field Marshal Rommel directly to Greece to take command ready for the invasion. German minesweepers and minelayers were transferred away from Sicily and additional minefields were laid off the Greek coast. Three panzer tank divisions were moved to Greece, two of them transferred from the Eastern Front, reducing the German forces fighting the Russians. The other division was withdrawn from France.

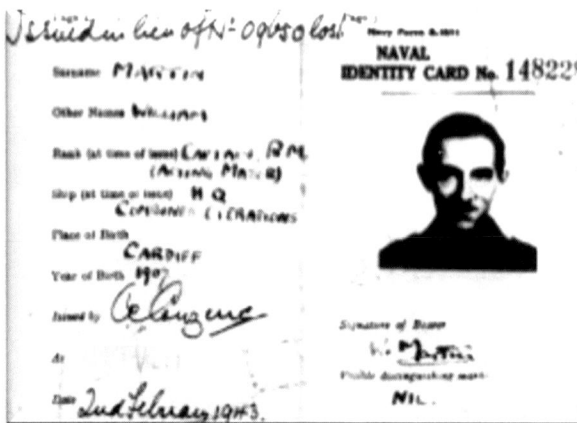

On the night of 9 July 1943 the Allies began the invasion of Sicily and by 17 August had achieved the strategic objective of driving the Axis forces from the island. Now the Mediterranean Sea lanes were open ready for the Allied invasion of mainland Italy. 'Operation Mincemeat' had successfully deceived the Germans and consequently saved countless Allied lives during the invasion of Sicily.

Chapter 11

Reconnaissance
By 1936 the RAF had developed cameras that allowed photos taken at high altitudes.

Espionage
In 1938 just before the outbreak of the war British Secret Service move to Station X

S.O.E

Prime Minister Winston Churchill authorises the S.O.E to 'set Europe ablaze' conducting ESPIONAGE and sabotage in enemy-held territories.

During the First World War of 1914 to 1918, Germany discovered that when they used the telegraph cable system for transmitting messages using Morse code, the British were able to intercept and decipher their messages. By the end of WWI a German engineer had developed an electro-mechanical cipher machine for coding messages, referred to as the Enigma machine. Messages could now be transmitted by wireless using only radio waves on long or short frequencies. Recipients expecting a message needed to be listening at certain times, which led to the development of fixed timed transmission schedules. During the 1920s electro-mechanical cipher machines were also used commercially and adopted by governments and military services of several countries, most notably by Nazi Germany from 1933.

In May 1938, a year before the outbreak of WWII, the head of the British Secret Intelligence Service (SIS) Admiral Sir Hugh Sinclair arranged the purchase of a mansion and grounds in rural Buckinghamshire on which planning permission had been granted for a housing estate. The property was to become the British secret service radio listening station, located away from London, hidden out of sight in countryside near the market town of Bletchley. The location had other advantages being within walking distance of a railway station, on what was known as the 'Varsity Line' connecting both Oxford and Cambridge. The line also joined the main West Coast railway system, giving Bletchley access to London, Birmingham, Manchester, Liverpool, and Edinburgh and Glasgow in Scotland. The Bletchley mansion was an ideal location tucked away in the English countryside. Existing admiralty and war office cryptanalysts moved from London to Bletchley in 1938 and a few days prior to the outbreak of WWII in September 1939 recruitment of further staff got under way in earnest. At first this worked by personal networking, particularly among those from the universities of Oxford and Cambridge. Others had a variety of backgrounds such as chess champions, crossword experts and linguist's fluency in German was especially required. With the German Abwehr now using electro-mechanical cipher machines for encrypting messages, formally trained mathematicians were also needed, as were experts in Morse code.

Specialists in telecommunications from the General Post Office were recruited to work at station 'BP', as it became commonly known. Many women were employed mainly for administrative and clerical jobs, and the site became a formal posting for many members of the Women's Royal Naval Service (WRNS)

The additional work space needed at station BP, was provided by erecting wooden huts in the grounds. Each had separate rooms, in which code breakers and analysts worked independently on separate tasks without necessarily knowing what the other huts did. All staff working at station BP had to sign the Official Secrets Act (1939) when joining. In 1942 a security warning to all members of staff emphasised the importance of discretion, even while working inside Bletchley itself: "Do not talk at meals. Do not talk in the transport travelling to work. Do not talk in your billet (accommodation) Do not talk by your own fireside. Be careful even in your Hut". The intelligence gained at station BP was considered in wartime Britain as the "**Ultra**" secret,   even higher than the former highest classification of 'Most Secret'. Security was paramount, since the Axis powers could not be allowed to know or even suspect that their Enigma codes could be or had been penetrated.

Landlocked between Germany and Russia, Poland was dependent on intelligence for its very survival. One Friday afternoon in 1930 a diplomatic package arrived at the Polish Postal service main sorting office in Warsaw for delivery to the German Embassy. Embassies were closed at weekends which meant the package had to remain at the postal service depot. That weekend, members of the Polish secret service opened the package, discovering it to be an electro-mechanical Enigma machine, but using the new disk rotor cipher system.

The Poles disassembled the machine, making diagrams and photographing the component parts, before reassembling and repackaging the Enigma for delivery along with the first post on the Monday morning to the German Embassy.

Polish cryptologists had been working deciphering secret German military text messages encrypted on Enigma machines for the previous few years, with the first being broken in December 1932. By 1938 with additional complexity repeatedly being added to Enigma machines, such as new rotor disks, made decryption far harder and increasing numbers of personnel and equipment were needed to enable codes to be broken quickly.

In August 1939 just five weeks before the Nazis invaded Poland at the outbreak of the war, the Polish Cipher Bureau revealed its achievements in breaking Enigma codes to both the British and French secret services - a stunning revelation. The Poles also handed over a cloned or copy machine that they had made.

By April 1941, a British cryptologist working at station BP realised that German weather ships, usually isolated and unprotected trawlers based in the North Atlantic near Iceland, were using Enigma codes for daily transmission of weather reports for German shipping. Transmitting Enigma messages like this meant that the trawlers would carry Enigma code books, to inform users how to set up the Enigma machines for each day's transmissions. In addition trawlers were in receipt of Kriegsmarine Enigma messages. In June 1941 the Royal Navy (RN) captured the German weather ship 'Lauenburg' near Iceland and the RN boarding party acquired important code books and parts of an Enigma machine from the ship before it was sunk. This material allowed The British cryptologist to further understand the Enigma codes, resulting in faster decoding of encrypted messages. Another big breakthrough came on the morning of 27 August 1941, when U-570, was attacked by HMS Bulldog and HMS Amethyst, both on patrol near Iceland. The U-boat was damaged by depth charges and forced to surface, causing the crew to abandon ship. The RN boarding party was then able to capture the U-boat Enigma machine together with code books, which were then sent to station BP. In May 1943 after the US joined the war a number of American cryptographers joined the staff at station BP and close co-operation between the British and American intelligence services was developed. However, the Soviet Union was never officially even told of the existence of station BP nor its activities.

When 'Ultra' information was passed over to Allied military commanders in the field, the information was always given a 'cover story' as to how it had been obtained for example from reconnaissance missions by agents or troops in an area. Intentionally visible to the enemy, the RAF would send spotter planes over enemy positions prior to an attack. The Germans would then assume their location had been discovered from the air, and not because **Enigma** codes had been compromised.

The work at station BP is estimated to have shortened the war by two years, and to have saved thousands of lives. By 1945 over 9000 people were working at Bletchley Park, all in total secrecy, unbeknown to their families or friends. Many took this secret to their grave.

Chapter 12

What planning?

August 1942 Carnage at Dieppe:

This was a total disaster.

The objectives of the ill-fated Dieppe raid in August 1942 were to seize and hold a major Axis seaport, if only for a short period; to prove that this was possible, and to gather intelligence, and then to destroy any coastal defences and port structures before retreating. The assault force consisted of some 240 ships that set sail from

Seaports along the southern coast of England on the evening of 18 August.

Unfortunately the Allied commanders were not aware that an Axis convoy had also sailed out from Boulogne along the French coast that same night heading for Dieppe. The convoy was spotted by British radar stations on the English coast as "unidentified vessels" and two warnings were then instantly radioed to the Allied assault force commanders. Sadly those warnings were not acknowledged nor was any evasive action taken. Consequently the inevitable happened as part of the Allied invasion armada ran into Axis armed trawlers escorting a large tanker. In the sea battle that developed the element of total surprise of the raid was lost. Catastrophically the vessels scheduled to arrive at Dieppe to assist the assault troops, by delivering the tanks in support of the infantry battalion, arrived too late.

The assault began at 5 a.m. but by 10:50 the Allied commanders were forced to call a retreat, when they were under very heavy fire. It became a total fiasco and tactical disaster. The withdrawal of the main landing force took three hours and was only completed by early afternoon. Of the 58 new Churchill tanks that had been adapted to operate in shallow water on the Dieppe beach in support of the infantry, two sank in the deep water and 12 more became bogged down in soft shingle on the beach itself. Only 15 tanks managed to cross the seawall and those that did were then confronted by a series of tank traps, purposely-built obstacles to prevent any armoured vehicles large or small entering the town.

After Dieppe, the triumphs, disasters and near misses of all Allied operations were scrutinised by CIU Medmenham, since the military planners had to consider all factors and eventualities when making plans for military operations.

A British Army officer Lieutenant-General Sir Frederick Morgan a graduate of the Royal Military Academy, Woolwich who had fought in both world wars and who escaped capture before being evacuated from Dunkirk in June 1940, was in charge of the department responsible for the successful planning of Operation Husky, the Allied invasion of Sicily. Plans for a full-scale assault on north Western Europe in what was to be known as Operation Overlord, officially began in earnest in 1943 within Sir Frederick Morgan's department.

Key factors governing selection of potential landing areas included the geology of its coastal location and the suitability for large-scale amphibious landings. Added to this were water depths, tides, currents, any natural geographical obstacles, and the proximity of any high ground or cliffs from which Axis forces could defend the area. The geological composition of the beaches, the sand itself, dunes, soft shale, quick sand, or any soft clay under the sand all were important in ensuring that chosen beaches would support the weight of tanks, heavy amour and other machinery. Beach gradients needed to be assessed as well as measuring the distance between high and low tides at any particular time of day. Just as vital were the areas directly behind potential invasion beaches and the potential to land airborne forces and to support and hold the ground against counter attack. The possible construction of forward landing grounds for aircraft was of particular importance. On top of all this the major factor was the feasibility of sending in supplies to the area, including for periods when an invasion force might become bogged down or halted.

After the declaration of war in September 1939, obtaining any up-to-date maps of Belgium and French coastal areas was out of the question. The most recent reliable maps were Michelin road maps drawn in 1938, which meant by 1942 these needed updating for the selection of potential major sites along the coast line. What planners also required was first-hand and reliable information from people on the ground in those areas about any recently built Axis fortifications. After becoming Prime Minister in June 1940, Winston Churchill instigated the

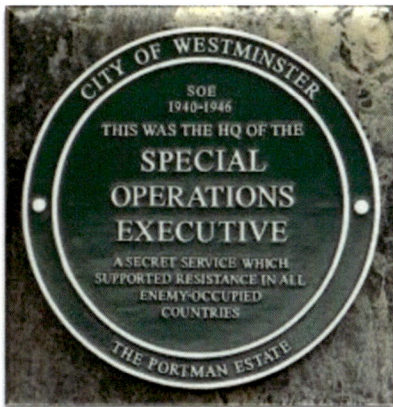

formation of the Special Operations Executive (SOE), to conduct espionage, sabotage and reconnaissance in occupied Europe against the Axis powers. In Churchill's own words he ordered SOE to "set Europe ablaze". Few people were aware of SOE's existence, even though it operated in all countries occupied by or attacked by the Axis forces.

A variety of people from different backgrounds and occupations joined SOE to operate in the underground occupied countries especially France, with numerous groups of resistance fighters under the control of SOE, along with SOE operatives living and working in France in strategic areas of importance who reported back directly to London. SOE operatives were called on to make reconnaissance reports on strategic areas such as coastal defences, railway marshalling yards and distribution centres.

On occasion resistance members were even able to get original copy plans of coastal fortifications. In one French town a member of the resistance, a painter and decorator by trade, was working in the planning office of the German Wehrmacht while painting the building. He was able to steal plans of the newly constructed coastal defences for that whole area and smuggle these out of the German headquarters. Such first-hand reconnaissance obtained by SOE agents along with photo reconnaissance, allowed military planners to build up substantial information about coastal areas. By mid-1943 RAF photographic reconnaissance missions were being flown almost daily along the French coast.

Updating maps with local geological and other information was paramount for planning for example this photo of the Remnants of the German U-boat Base in Bordeaux.

Chapter 13

Reconnaissance.

Knowing your enemy's intentions without the enemy knowing necessitates espionage mainly done in the form of reconnaissance, secretly looking without being caught spying on; and where possible taking photos.

By the 1930s the RAF had developed an electrical heating system for cameras that allowed reconnaissance aircraft to take pictures from very high altitudes without the camera's moving parts freezing up. During the war, the Super Marine Spitfire, a single-seated fighter aircraft designed by the British aeronautical engineer Reginald J. Mitchell, combat-ready and complete with all armaments, ammunition and radio equipment could reach top speeds of around 330 mph. Removing all the armaments, and fitting larger fuel tanks, even when fitted with five heated reconnaissance cameras the plane could reach a maximum speed of 396 mph.

In September 1939, the RAF formally took control of a civilian photo reconnaissance unit based at Heston Aerodrome in the Twickenham area of London. This unit had previously been contracted by British SIS to perform clandestine photographic reconnaissance over Europe. In November 1940 the unit became the RAF Photographic Reconnaissance Unit and the Spitfire camouflaged to avoid detection, became one of the first high-speed aircraft to be used for this work. The unarmed planes flew at high, medium and low altitudes, often ranging far into enemy territory to observe the Axis powers and throughout the war provided an almost continual flow of valuable intelligence information, especially of Axis installations.

In April 1941 the RAF photographic interpretation unit (PIU) moved from the Wembley area of London to a new home at Danesfield House, in Medmenham in the rural countryside of Buckinghamshire near Henley-on-Thames just about 45 miles away from Station X. Soon after moving, the unit was renamed the Central Interpretation Unit (CIU). Its work was classified 'most secret' during 1942 and 1943, as the CIU gradually expanded and was involved in the planning stages of practically every operation of the war, and in every aspect of intelligence. The art of examining photographic images for the purpose of identifying objects and judging their significance was not a new idea.

However examining two identical photos of the same image using a Stereoscope, a simple optical instrument comprising of two lenses gives the viewer the optical illusion of a three-dimensional image.

This technique was of particular significance to the work at RAF Medmenham. With a Stereoscope the interpreter was able to calculate the size, height and depth of a shape or shadow as well as the geographical situation of the object. This most basic principle of image interpretation made RAF Medmenham the main interpretation centre for photographic reconnaissance operations in the European and Mediterranean theatres of war. Later, the Bomber Command Damage Assessment Section was amalgamated with CIU. Up to 150 women were employed on photographic interpretation and by the end of the war over 1,700 personnel were working at the unit.

The second front opened on the night of 9-10 July 1943 with the Allied invasion of Sicily, codenamed Operation Husky. Ending on 17 August, the operation achieved all the strategic goals set by the planners, an amphibious assault on the island by two armies, one landing on the south eastern and the second on the central southern coast. Canadian Prime Minister, Mackenzie King, along with Canadian military leaders in England, had insisted that Canada should participate in the invasion and it was agreed that the 1st Canadian Infantry Division should be included in the plans, finalised in late April 1943, with the approval of General Andrew McNaughton commander of the First Canadian Army.

After 38 days, the Allies drove the Axis forces out from Sicily, and then moved into mainland Italy, thus opening up 'the second front'. On 24 July 1943, soon after the start of the invasion of mainland Italy in the Calabria region, the Italian dictator Benito Mussolini was toppled from power, when the king of Italy, Victor Emmanuel III had Mussolini arrested and imprisoned.

As can be seen from this recent map; entrance to the Mediterranean Sea, is via the Strait of Gibraltar or by the Suez Canal both of these being British Colony's during WWII. Malta an archipelago in the central Mediterranean sea between Sicily and the North African coast. (In 1814 Malta became a crown colony of the British Empire, and remained until granted independence in 1964). Germany and Italy realised the strategical importance of this British colony just some 103 miles south from Sicily. This was the home of the British Navy's Mediterranean fleet. From 1940 to 1942 the Axis powers put Malta under siege, attacking both the RAF bases on the island as well as the Royal Navy Dock yards and constantly bombing Malta's ports, towns, and cities. This included attacking the Allied shipping convoys, bringing supplies of food, materials and fuel to the island hoping to starve and force the people of Malta into submission.   Malta was the most bombed place during WWII more than 14,000 bombs were dropped, destroying about 30,000 buildings but Malta still fought on. On 15 April 1942 King George VI awarded the people of Malta the George Cross in appreciation of their heroism.   **Malta G.C.**

On 8 September 1943 Italy signed the 'Armistice of Cassibile' and quit the Axis powers. Italy was then plunged into civil war, with some Italian forces joining the Allies, and others remaining loyal to Mussolini and the Axis forces in fighting on against the Allies. The huge amphibious invasion from Tunisia into Sicily in the southern Mediterranean made it easer for the Allies to transfer forces into mainland Europe using Sicily as a stepping stone, especially when the Allies could depend on air support from some 600 fighter aircraft based on the British island of Malta, south of Sicily as well as the Allied air bases in North Africa.

Chapter 14   Quadrant Conference.

Quadrant was the codename given to the highly secret military conference held in August 1943 attended by British **Prime minister** Churchill and American President Roosevelt hosted by Canadian Prime Minister, Mackenzie King in the city of Quebec, to discuss the Allies, future military strategy.

The American delegation wanted a direct invasion into France that year, whereas Winston Churchill wanted to invade Italy, which he called 'the soft underbelly of the Axis'. At previous meetings, Churchill had succeeded in delaying the date for any direct landing in France, to allow time to build up more resources in the United Kingdom prior to any invasion.

Because the Allied forces had already invaded Sicily the month before during the conference, news arrived of Italy's impending surrender. There was now a real possibility of establishing an Allied front in northern Italy, close to Germany. Eisenhower had authorised the invasion into the Italian mainland with the purpose of diverting German forces away from, or out of France, so as to open up a second front.

The Allies also agreed and decided that a cross-channel attack into France codename Overlord, was to be the main Anglo-American effort in Europe for 1944, and set a provisional target date of May. The conference also discussed an increase in the bombing offensive against Germany and a continued buildup of American forces and resources in Britain prior to any cross-channel invasion.

The UK and USA also agreed that neither would use the new nuclear weapons that were by now in rapid development, nor would they communicate any nuclear intelligence to a third party without mutual consent.

At this time support for the war among the Italian public was declining and Churchill believed that an invasion on to the mainland would remove Italy from the Axis forces in the Mediterranean.

This would open up the Mediterranean's shipping lanes to all Allied vessels, in turn reducing the amount of shipping capacity needed to supply Allied forces in the Middle East and the Far East at a critical time when the availability of Allied shipping capacity was in short supply.

Relief to shipping capacity would also enable increased British and American supplies to the Soviet Union, at the same time tying down German forces and keeping them away from the Russian front.

The Joint Allied Forces Headquarters (AFHQ) established in August 1942 with its HQ in London under General Dwight Eisenhower was now operationally responsible for all Allied land forces in the Mediterranean theatre. AFHQ planned and commanded the invasion of the Italian mainland codenamed Operation Avalanche.

On 3 September 1943 the first phase commenced with the British Eighth Army, led by General Montgomery crossing the Straits of Messina from Sicily to Reggio di Calabria on the toe of the Italian mainland. At the same time 1st Canadian Infantry Division landed at Cape Spartivento on the southern coast. Opposition to these landings was light, as local Italian units surrendered almost immediately. The secret Armistice of Cassibile signed in the village of Cassibile in Sicily on the 3 September although not made public until the 8 September, presented a total capitulation of Italy once authorised by King Victor Emanuel III and the Italian Prime Minister Pietro Badoglio.

On 9 September the main invasion force landed around Salerno on the west coast of Italy, an area selected as closer to air bases, established on Sicily during the four-week Allied occupation. The Salerno coast had good tidal conditions for sea landings since transport vessels could anchor close to its narrow beaches. During the surrender negotiations the Italian government offered to open the ports of Taranto and Brindisi on Italy's eastern coast, where German forces were very weak. Supreme Allied Commander General Eisenhower quickly planned a third landing, codenamed Slapstick, to take advantage of this offer.

Also on 9 September, the British 1 Airborne Division landed at Taranto after crossing the Mediterranean in four Royal Navy cruisers, their decks loaded with the division's vehicles and supplies from North Africa. On 8 September, while the convoy was at sea, General Eisenhower broadcast details of the Italian surrender. As the Allied flotilla approached Taranto, home of the Italian Navy two Italian battleships and three cruisers were seen leaving the harbour sailing to Malta to surrender in accordance with the agreement between the Allies and the Italian government.

The first units ashore were the headquarters of the 4th Parachute Brigade and the 10th Parachute Battalion, which were directed to move inland to guard against any German attack. Airborne troops entering the city, were welcomed by the Italian defenders who informed them that German forces had already departed, which was why the landing's had been unopposed. Taranto's main value was it was a large port and still in full working order.

The only German forces left in the region were units of the First Fallschirmjäger Division, who engaged the Allies with ambushes and roadblocks, frustrating attempts to advance north towards Rome. Fighting was particularly fierce at Monte Cassino, a historic Benedictine hilltop abbey, which the Allies were convinced that the Germans were using as an artillery observation point for the surrounding area.

The abbey's stone walls, 150 feet high and 10 feet thick, made it virtually impregnable to Allied field engineers. Eventually the Allies were forced to bomb the abbey with 1,150 tons of high explosives, reducing Monte Cassino to a smoking mass of rubble. This became prime fighting positions and allowed the Germans to hold out for a further 123 days against repeated assaults and heavy bombardment by the Allies. Monte Cassino was finally taken by Polish troops who fought their way up the heights to raise a Polish flag over the ruins. Only at this point was the road to Rome open for the Allies to advance and liberate the city, which they achieved on the 4 June 1944, just two days before the Normandy invasion. Unfortunately the Allies failed to take full advantage of the Italian armistice and Italian troops were rapidly replaced by German Wehrmacht divisions taken from other European theatres of war.

The battle for Italy was not over.

Chapter 15   Beach Obstacles.

The first obstacles to be found prior to reaching any invasion beach area along the French coastline and at other potential landing points were large formations of floating sea-mines laid by the Kriegsmarine (as illustration). There were different types of sea-mines, all moored by metal cables to the sea bed. If contact was made with the 'horns' on the mine it would detonate. Mines would also be laid deep in the water in the shipping lanes, unable to be seen from ships. These sea-mines were aimed at larger ships and any vessel whose draft meant it floated deep in the water. Other mines would be laid just under the surface targeting smaller boats and ships with shallow hulls. Some mines were laid visibly floating on the surface.

From the high ground overlooking the beaches.

Beach Obstacles

As well as mine-fields out at sea, the approaches to the beaches themselves had a variety of obstacles aimed at destroying or delaying any invasion craft getting to the beaches in order to land troops or unload equipment to support troops already on the beaches.

These included angled steel structure welded together from triangular steel bars, their ends sharpened to penetrate the hull of landing craft. These obstacles were positioned at the water's edge just below the high tide point, some anchored in concrete.

Posts with pressure mines fixed on top were sited at the low tide mark. When visible craft trying to avoid contact would be forced to slow down and be in range of machine gun or mortar fire from German defenders.

At the low tide water's edge, tree trunks were positioned like tripods sunk deep into the beach and fitted with sharp metal blades or iron bars to rip open the hulls of vessels that collided with them. Some tripods would also have pressure mines attached that detonated on contact with landing craft.

Between the high tide line and the first line of obstacles the Germans placed vehicle pressure mines placed under the sand. These were inter-linked, so that if one mine was activated it would detonate other mines in a random pattern.

Anti-personnel mines were also placed in these areas, which when trodden on or activated by trip-wires some would spring up out from the ground to a height of about one metre before detonating, blasting splinters of metal shrapnel or ball bearings over a wide area. These mines earned the nickname Bouncing Bettys by some Allied troops.

Their effect was devastating since they caused horrific wounds all part of the psychological warfare to lower the morale of invading troops and to slow them down when crossing the 'killing ground' that was well within the range of machine gun and mortar fire from defending German troops.

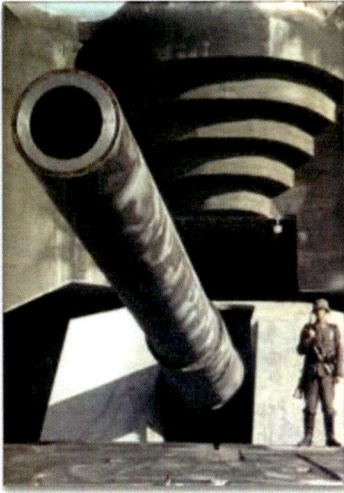

As part of the Atlantic Wall along the exposed French coastline inland at high vantage points overlooking the sea, the Germans built large gun emplacements. Some were equipped with large self-propelled-guns with the range to fire out to sea to a distance of some fourteen to sixteen miles, accurately targeting approaching ships. The gun emplacements prominently positioned on top of the 100-foot-high cliffs on the 'Pointe du Hoc' peninsular in Normandy overlooking the English Channel were especially heavily fortified in 1943. As the highest point on this the Normandy coastline overlooking two beaches, the guns presented a significant threat to Allied ships out at sea or approaching, as well as any vessels anchored offshore, giving firing support to the invasion force in their landing craft approaching the beaches.

At the approaches and exits to beaches, fortified concrete positions were constructed to accommodate both artillery and anti-tank guns as well as to protect the batteries of machine guns aimed directly onto the beaches. Cut deep into the landscape giving them added protection and concealment from attacking forces off the beaches, these fortifications were festooned with barbed wire entanglements.

Between the beaches and approach roads, as part of the Atlantic Wall, the Germans constructed defensive rows of concrete 'Dragon teeth' and other similar anti-tank traps to prevent invaders breaking out from coastal areas and moving inland. In addition to these fortifications, millions of mines were laid all along the coastal defences immediately inland along the Atlantic Wall area. Rommel's defensive strategy was that any Allied invasion must be met at the Atlantic Wall, then pinned down and held at the beachheads by what he called 'static divisions' manning the forts. They then would be hit by a mobile reserve force of Panzer divisions held inland' ready to counter-attack the invasion.

Rommel predicted that if the Allies could not be stopped and held on the beaches, the Axis forces would lose the war.

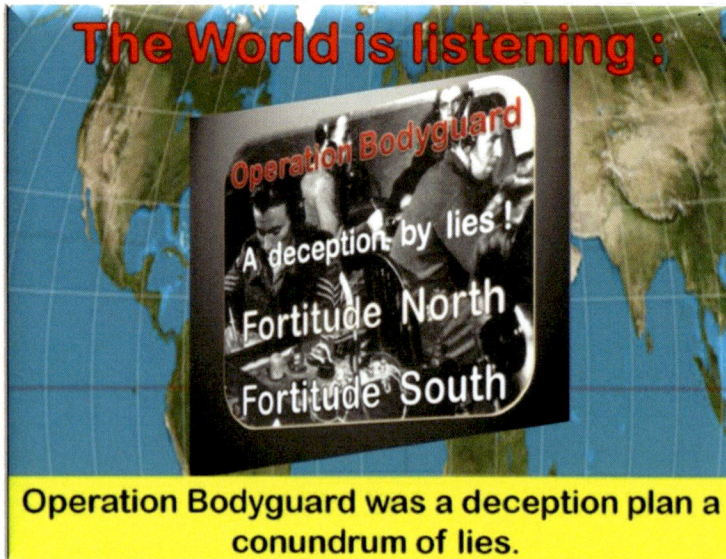

The World is listening :

Operation Bodyguard

A deception by lies !

Fortitude North

Fortitude South

Operation Bodyguard was a deception plan a conundrum of lies.

By December 1943 it was estimated that one million American service personnel were based in Great Britain, the great majority being men. However there were many female clerks, doctors, drivers, nurses and Red Cross staff to organise the welfare and social programme for American troops now based away from home. This figure also included female members of the clandestine Office of Strategic Services (OSS) that the United States intelligence agency had formed the previous year.

Britain was now effectively an island ordnance and transport depot, stock piled with every conceivable piece of equipment in secret military depots at strategically placed locations throughout the country, ready for the anticipated invasion of mainland Europe. One such depot, established in 1940, was at Thatcham, a small town in Berkshire, three miles east of Newbury where I lived and fifteen miles west of Reading, accessible by main roads in the Thames valley and linked by railway to London and the south-west of England. A few miles south of Thatcham the MOD Ministry of Defence in 1942 built Greenham Common RAF base. This was now turned over to the USAAF and referred to as station AAF-486 for security reasons, and used by the American Ninth Army Air Force for fighter groups arriving from America as well as a troop carrier base for troops arriving in Britain during 1943.

The Allies came up with a deception strategy, code named Bodyguard, to prevent the actual location for the invasion leaking out during the build-up period. The main risk was German Abwehr spies that the British Security Service, MI5, was not aware of but who could still be based in Britain.

Under the Bodyguard plan, (but on paper only), two large field armies were created initially: Fortitude North based in Scotland and Fortitude South based in Kent opposite the Pas de Calais.

To the east of London across the Thames estuary in Essex and in Cambridgeshire, Norfolk and Suffolk the USAAF had over 70 airbases housing some sixty thousand service personnel. The increased bombing offensive against Germany agreed at the Quadrant conference by USAAF and the RAF came from these bases. The Abwehr knew therefore that the area was saturated with military bases, as well as the RAF bases in the south of England the Germans had attacked during the Battle of Britain in the summer and autumn of 1940. During WWII, a field army comprised two or more army corps such as Royal Artillery, Tank or Signals corps. A field army usually had around a strength of 80,000 combatants under the command of a General.

Fortitude North

One of these fake armies, Fortitude North based in Edinburgh would account for my father's unit '22 Beach Recovery' being away over Christmas 1943, in Scotland on exercise "Roundabout II".

Although genuinely in support of the Canadian Armoured Corps he was in

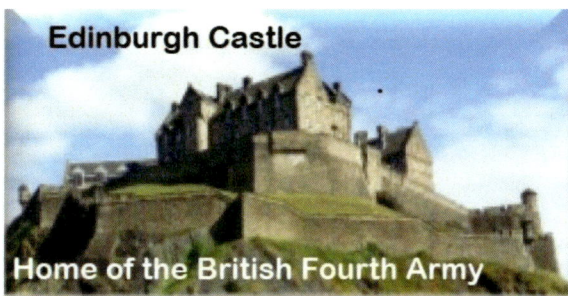
Edinburgh Castle
Home of the British Fourth Army

reality a part of the Bodyguard 'bluff'. When the Abwehr listened in to messages between signals units of Fortitude north, in reality they were listening only to messages from bogus units. But from a build-up of wireless communications the Abwehr deduced the Allies were preparing an invasion of Norway at Trondheim. Additional extra high frequency transmissions between fake units with false information about the arrival of non-existent troops in the area were also supported by the BBC which broadcast fake names, such as the results of football matches between these non-existent regiments being played at towns in Scotland. This deception worked very well: Hitler built up thirteen army divisions in Norway to counter an invasion by Fortitude North. Edinburgh was bombed 28 times during World War II.

Fortitude South was to consist of two army groups, the 21st Army Group, a British headquarters formation, two field armies and other supporting units, consisting primarily of both British and Canadian forces all under the command of General Montgomery. Montgomery had been critical of what he perceived as a strategic muddle in the Italian campaign and was glad to return to England on the 23 December 1943, the same time as '22 Beach Recovery Unit' was sent to Scotland.

Fortitude South
English Channel

FIRST UNITED STATES ARMY GROUP

The First United States Army Group (FUSAG) this was another 'phantom' formation existing only on paper, but notably under the command of General Patton, who had been called back to London from the Italian campaign. The planned deception was that Fortitude South would invade the Pas de Calais, the shortest crossing of the English Channel and therefore the most direct route into Germany.   As opposed to over Scotland, the Luftwaffe still had the ability to fly reconnaissance missions over the south of England, despite heavy losses in the previous two years and its ongoing daily commitment defending Germany against Allied daylight bombing raids.   There remained a need to sell the deception that Fortitude South's invasion would be in the Pas de Calais area.

However at no stage were the Abwehr fed false documents or invasion plans with maps, as had been the case with Operation Mincemeat. Instead through disinformation they deduced and concluded for themselves the Pas de Calais to be the invasion area. A massive invasion into Europe would need wide expanses of beach on which to land any invading forces.

Decoy inflatable equipment

Placing FUSAG in the south-east of England and directly opposite Calais, the Abwehr who regarded General Patton as the top allied general, reckoned his army would lead the invasion. To strengthen and encourage this belief the Allies left decoy equipment out in the area, for any Luftwaffe reconnaissance planes to find.   General Patton visited Dover and the Kent area on several occasions inspecting military establishments, always with members of the Press taking photos and reporting for publication back in the United States, where the OSS knew the Abwehr had agents working in the so-called neutral embassies. Bodyguard's programme of deception required the support of many organisations, all without divulging the actual location for operation Overlord that by December 1943 was still known by only a very few Senior Ranks.

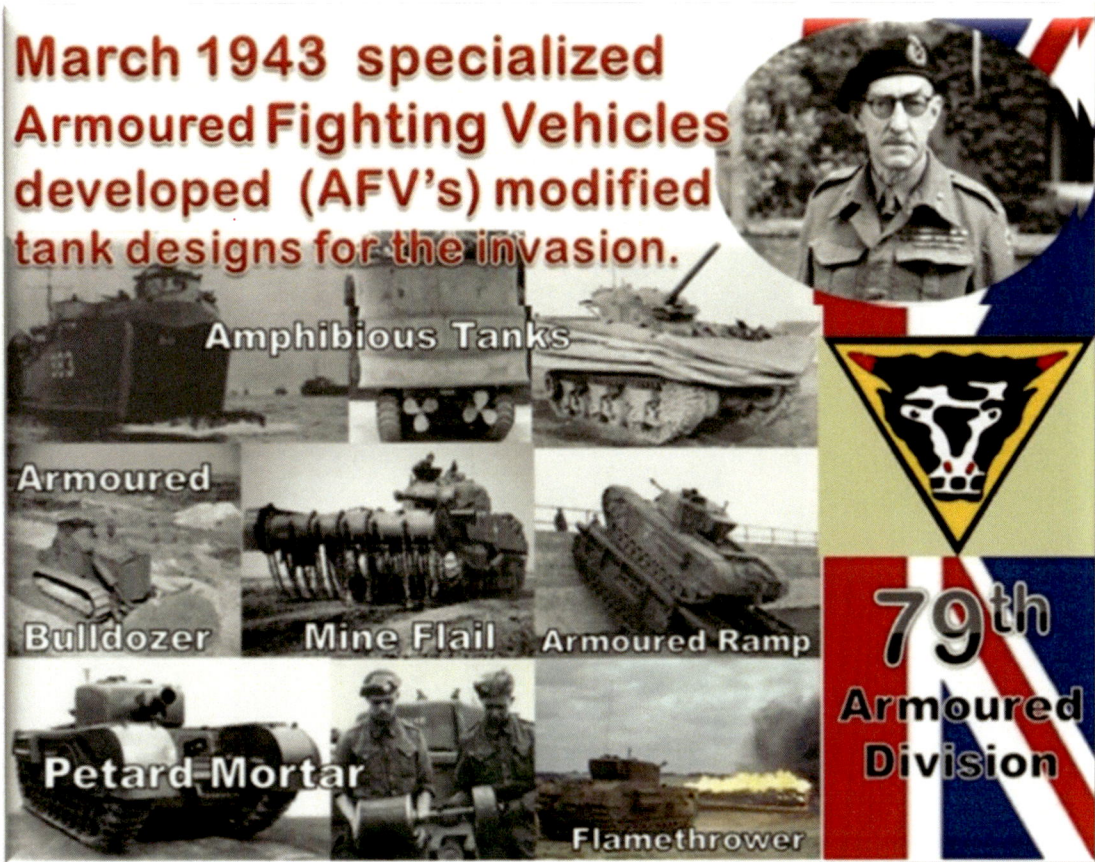

March 1943 specialized Armoured Fighting Vehicles developed (AFV's) modified tank designs for the invasion.

Amphibious Tanks

Armoured Bulldozer

Mine Flail

Armoured Ramp

Petard-Mortar

Flamethrower

79th Armoured Division

In 1941 it was brought to Winston Churchill's attention by a military historian that a British tank expert, a major-general who had been dismissed into retirement in 1940, was serving as a volunteer lance-corporal in the Local Defence Volunteers in a small rural town in Gloucestershire. Prior to his enforced retirement Percy Hobart served in the British Army in Egypt where he was Director of Military Training for Armoured Fighting Vehicles, (AFVs). However, his ideas about armoured warfare had not been appreciated by the old guard of cavalry staff officers now based at the war office in London. Churchill immediately had Hobart re-enlisted with the rank of general and assigned him to raise and train a fresh armoured division The 79th Armoured Division.

Lessons had been learnt from the disaster of the Dieppe landings in 1942 when tanks that had been adapted to operate in shallow water still got bogged down in soft shingle, or sank in deep water. Tank traps and other obstacles that prevented vehicles getting away from the beach areas had shown the need for specialised vehicles to cope with such obstructions during an invasion.

In March 1943 Hobart was asked to convert his division into units of specialized armour of modified tank designs. Collectively these became known as 'Hobart's Funnies'.

One was the Sherman flail tank developed to clear both mines and wire entanglements using a rotating cylinder of weighted chains that flailed the ground in front of the tank exploding any mines in its path. The flail tank had been developed from a prototype used during the North African campaign to cut pathways through Axis minefields.

Another conversion was the armoured bulldozer developed by the British army, a conventional D8 Caterpillar fitted with armour to protect both the driver and the engine. After mine clearance these could then be used to clear other obstacles and prepare the exits from the beaches. Initially operated by the British 79th Armoured Division in support of armoured assaults, the bulldozer was used by combat engineers in the latter months of the war.

The explosive projectile

The Churchill tanks main armament could be replaced by a Petard Mortar that fired a forty-pound high explosive projectile nicknamed the 'Flying dustbin'. From a distance of some 150 yards it was capable of destroying concrete obstacles such as roadblocks and bunkers. The projectile was loaded and primed externally, by opening a hatch and sliding the projectile into the mortar usually by an NCO from the Royal Engineers who was a specialist in demolitions.

These are just three examples of Armoured Fighting Vehicles (AFVs). Others did exist however the other notable Vehicle to mention is the BAVR. This was designed specifically for the Beach Recovery Sections:

Experience gained from the Allied invasions of North Africa, Sicily and on the west coast of Italy at Salerno, showed that armoured vehicles could not simply be charged off landing craft and into battle; in fact they had to be trundled off at low speed. When stalled or swamped by surf or tides, there was then an urgent need to clear these landing vessels out of the way so as not to block beach entrances and exits. Damaged vehicles if left submerged could impede any incoming craft, so they needed immediately to be cleared and towed away.

These tasks were assigned to Beach Recovery Sections whose REME personnel had been developing a Beach Armoured Recovery Vehicle for this specific purpose. Its other function was to push any stranded landing craft off the beach after they had unloaded.

The BARV had a crew of five including one diver who connected the towing cables to vehicles at various points which were often underwater. The BARV was approximately 23 feet long and 8½ feet wide and weighed 30 tons.

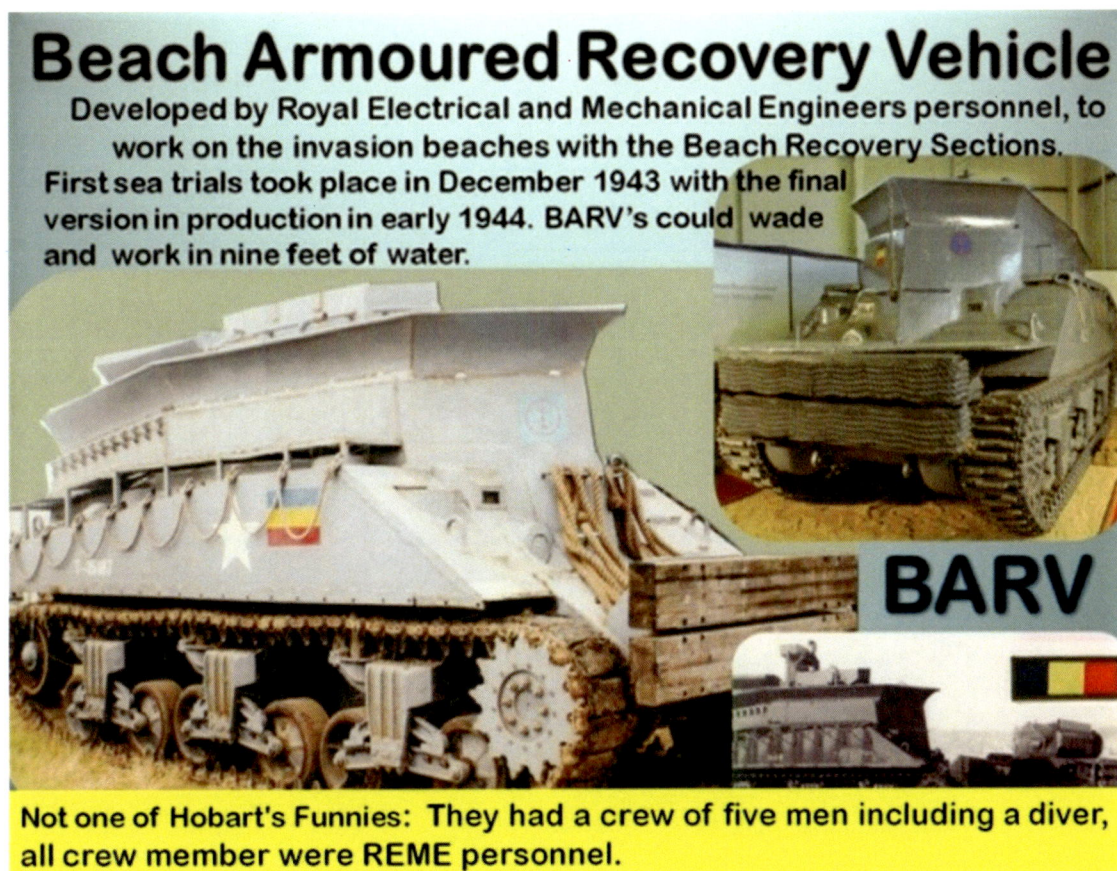

Beach Armoured Recovery Vehicle
Developed by Royal Electrical and Mechanical Engineers personnel, to work on the invasion beaches with the Beach Recovery Sections. First sea trials took place in December 1943 with the final version in production in early 1944. BARV's could wade and work in nine feet of water.

BARV

Not one of Hobart's Funnies: They had a crew of five men including a diver, all crew member were REME personnel.

'Logistics' is the management of the flow of goods between the point of origin and the point of consumption. Military planners were only too aware of this fact in their preparation and planning for supplying the armies of an invasion force. If nothing else, the disaster at Dieppe in 1942 proved that the Allies could not rely on capturing a sea port intact and in full working order. To keep an invading army supplied on mainland Europe, the Allies would need a deep water port with dockside cranes able to accommodate ocean-going cargo ships transporting bulky cargoes of stores and equipment. A vice-admiral on the Overlord planning committee suggested: 'If a port could not be captured then one should be taken across the channel?' He meant with the invaders. At a later planning meeting Winston Churchill recalled that in 1917, during WWI, he had imagined a similar scenario using captured German islands with considered redundant ships sunk to form a bridgehead for an invasion. The idea was sold and accepted by planners for the creation of the Allies' own floating harbour or port. The idea of concrete structures able to float was not a new idea; during WWI concrete ships and barges were built when American steel shipbuilders were full to capacity.

Secret Technology **Mulberry Harbours**

A vice-admiral on the Overlord planning committee suggested;
If a port could not be captured then one should be taken across the channel with the invaders.

Concrete formed into caissons, a watertight retaining structure that provided buoyancy could be constructed in sections, floated across the English Channel and then sunk into place to make a port.

The average sized of a caisson was 65 yards long, by 20 yards high by 10 yards wide.

At the height of production in late summer 1943 some 45,000 people were employed on this project. It was so secret that even those working on it were unaware of its true purpose.

Nothing consumes fuel, including petrol, faster than AFVs, especially tanks, as nothing moved except by mechanical means. Petroleum became a priceless commodity in wartime. Keeping the Allied invasion forces on the move required a constant supply of Petroleum fuels and lubricants, without which any advance would at best slow down and at worst grind to a halt. Motor fuels from England would be the highest priority for the Allies.

Early in the war it was realised that oil storage depots located near English Channel sea ports would be vulnerable to attack by the Luftwaffe. Therefore planners were already looking at ways of using a pipe line system to carry fuel from safer storage facilities around Bristol and Liverpool down to the English Channel ports. Operation **Pluto** (Pipe-Lines under the Ocean) was the project conceived to relieve dependence on oil tankers, which could be slowed by bad weather and susceptible to attack by both the Luftwaffe and or Kriegsmarine submarines. If telephone cables could be laid across the Atlantic Ocean then a pipeline could be laid across the English Channel.

Secret Technology

P.L.U.T.O

Weymouth   Isl

Bambi

Cherbourg

Sark

Tanks require a constant supply of petrol and oil when in battle, it must be available on demand.

Operation Pluto (Pipe-Lines Under The Ocean) was conceived to relieve dependence and susceptible to submarines. Ocean then a on oil tankers, that could be slowed by bad weathe attack by both the Luftwaffe and or Kriegsmarine If telephone cables could be laid across the Atlanti pipeline could be laid across the English Channel.

Nine weeks after D-Day on 12 August 1944 the first pipe line was laid from Shanklin Chine on the Isle of Wight across the English Channel to Cherbourg.

Pipe-Line-Under-The- Ocean

Chapter 19.   A Dry Run!

Those amphibious landings at both Dieppe and Sicily proved that assault forces require overwhelming fire support from self-propelled artillery landing as part of the forward infantry, together with their own tanks supported by AFV's of all types. A vast number of vehicles of all shapes and sizes formed the vanguard of an assault. After leaving the comparative safety of a dry environment on board their transporting vessels all these vehicles would sooner or later on leaving have to negotiate open beaches. Here they could be susceptible to water from rising tides, freak waves caused by high winds, or explosions out at sea. Unloading could not be carried out only at low tide but had to be ongoing. So realistically any vehicle arriving on a beach could one minute have its engine operating in an ideal dry condition but the next find itself immersed in sea water. A waterproofing programme was paramount and needed to be implemented urgently.

I quote now from Colonel Murray C. Johnston book CANADA'S CRAFTSMEN AT 50! The Story of Electrical and Mechanical Engineering regiment of Canada after their first fifty years anniversary.

There were four main categories of waterproofing materials: hardware such as ventilation stacks or air intake tubes; prepared plastic compounds; adhesives which usually had a synthetic rubber base; and preservatives such as paints, greases and waterproof cloths. Thousands of tons of these materials were made up into kits each designed for a specific vehicle or equipment. Each kit included illustrated directions for waterproofing. This waterproofing process was carried out in three stages, the first involving inspection, maintenance, checks and general sealing of fixtures such as hull turret rings. The second stage was carried out at marshalling areas and involved the final erection and fitting of hardware, adjustments and final sealing of fixtures. The third and final stage was done at embarkation and involved sealing of access ports, track lubrication and fitting of tow ropes.

(This gives a glimpse of the size of the task involved with the waterproofing of all vehicles.)

M.F.M.4.records: On 12 February 1944 my father was recalled back to the first Canadian Base Workshop located at Bordon camp in Hampshire. Febuary 1944 saw the birth of a new regiment in the history of Canada, at least on paper: after all the official ceremonial protocols were carried out and documented, only then could it officially come into being as it did on 15 May 1944.

The regiment was the result of the fusion of all the various elements of the Royal Canadian Army service Corps, Royal Canadian Engineers, and various trades of the Royal Canadian Ordnance Corps. Once in existence, the Royal Canadian Electrical and Mechanical Engineers' role was to train and deploy specialists in response to demand, including situations such as the waterproofing programme.

The Emergency Powers (Defence Act) of August 1938 empowered the British government to take certain measures in the defence of the nation: One such power was requisitioning, (meaning to officially take or use) property or goods during the war for the benefit of the war effort.

At their meeting in Casablanca in January 1943, Roosevelt and Churchill had agreed to the setting up of a joint allied team of planners for this operation, named Overlord. In December that year Roosevelt appointed the American General Eisenhower as Chief of Staff Supreme Allied Commander (COSSAC). General Eisenhower believed that all invasion training had to be carried out in conditions as near to real battle conditions as possible to accustom troops and to expose them to all situations. This led to the requisitioning of various venues for this training.

One was the small farming village of Imber in Wiltshire on Salisbury Plain in the south of England. On 1 November 1943, the villagers were called to a meeting in the village schoolroom and given forty-seven days' notice to leave their homes. The village was to be used by American forces to practise street fighting and house clearance. Some seventy five years later, Imber is still used as a training ground for urban warfare by British military forces. As a boy cadet in July 1962 I trained there on Urban Warfare exercises.

Another area requisitioned and turned over to the American forces in late 1943 was an area to the west of Lyme Bay - the beaches at Slapton Sands in Devon. Again, the local residents, some 3000, were evacuated. The first of these training exercises was carried out in December 1943. Such realistic rehearsals gave American forces the opportunity to familiarise themselves with boarding and disembarking from the various types of landing craft, infantry and landing ship, tanks and other vessels.

As the months progressed into 1944, one such exercise was 'Operation Tiger', a phase of exercise 'Fabius' and planned on a large scale, with thousands of American troops from the fourth infantry division participating. Live firing had been organised to make the exercise even more realistic: HMS Hawkins, a British heavy cruiser, was to shell the beach with live ammunition for 30 minutes prior to the actual landings.

Because some of the landing ships were delayed in arriving, the live firing exercise was rescheduled to commence later than the originally planned time. Unfortunately some of the landing craft did not receive the rescheduled timings, with the result that troops were landing on the beach at the same time as the bombardment took place - straight into so-called 'friendly fire'.

To compound this tragedy, in the early hours of the following morning the

American convoy of follow up troops, was attacked in Lyme Bay by nine German E-boats. British ships had sighted the E-boats earlier that night but because the LSTs and British naval headquarters were operating on different radio frequencies, the American forces could not be warned.

American ship LST-325 at Slapton Sands Devon in April 1944.

For nearly 40 years, well after the end of the war, Operation Tiger remained a secret. Today on the beaches of Slapton Sands, there remains a small memorial to the 946 men who lost their lives.

The supreme commander of forces in the air, on the ground and at sea, was just one man orchestrating all three Allied forces. By 1943 the largest of the Allied forces were the Americans. Because of this, and due to his handling of operation Torch, part of the North African campaign from 1942 onwards, President Roosevelt appointed Dwight David Eisenhower nicknamed 'Ike' as the Supreme Allied Commander in Europe for operation Overlord.

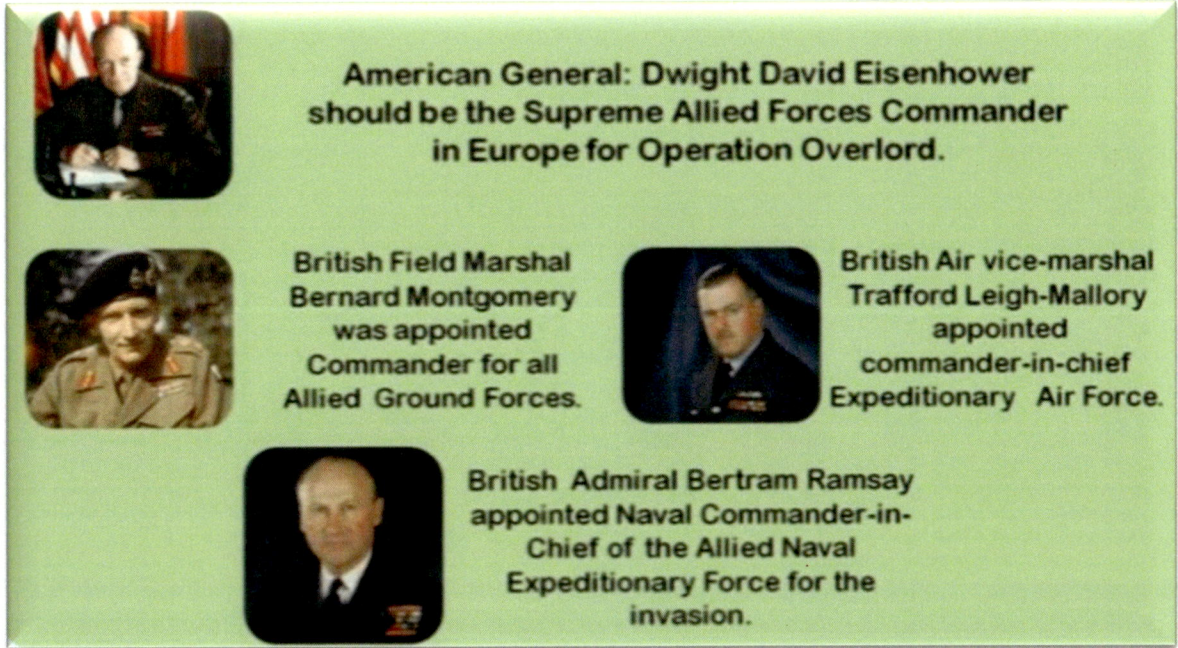

American General: Dwight David Eisenhower should be the Supreme Allied Forces Commander in Europe for Operation Overlord.

British Field Marshal Bernard Montgomery was appointed Commander for all Allied Ground Forces.

British Air vice-marshal Trafford Leigh-Mallory appointed commander-in-chief Expeditionary Air Force.

British Admiral Bertram Ramsay appointed Naval Commander-in-Chief of the Allied Naval Expeditionary Force for the invasion.

During 1943 the COSSAC team had drawn up battle plans for Overlord. However it was not until January 1944 that this team first met together in Britain. Montgomery and Eisenhower amended the original plans by increasing the ground force from three to five divisions and supported by three airborne divisions, not just two one on each flank.

A division consists of about 30,000 soldiers, and tends to be the smallest combined army unit. It is, never the less, capable of independent operations, having a wide and varied range of combat troops with their own support units.

Increasing the number of land divisions from three to five increased the area required for landing. A much wider beach area was now required. This in turn would allow for a much quicker buildup of forces on to the beach head. However this increase of troops meant that bigger numbers of amphibious vessels would be needed to transport troops to the beaches.

The landings at Anzio, part of the Italian campaign that started in January 1944, was seen as a debacle, since it took many days to clear troops from the landing ships onto the beach. Subsequently this meant that the amphibious landing craft and troop carriers used at Anzio could not get back to the English Channel as originally scheduled to be used for operation Overlord.

Winston Churchill was clearly displeased with this action stating, "I had hoped we were hurling a wildcat onto the shore at Anzio, but all we got was a stranded whale". This delay meant operation Overlord could not get under way until the end of May 1944 at the earliest.

By April, Eisenhower had complete control of the Allied air force and was able to switch concentrated daylight bombing raids against Germany to targets in France, not only in the Normandy area but against all road and rail links into Normandy. Not all bombing was concentrated in Normandy, as this could have revealed that the intended Allied invasion was not the Pas de Calais area. Eisenhower concentrated crippling bombing attacks on all Luftwaffe air bases throughout northern France, as well as paralysing rail links in the area. Failure at Dieppe had highlighted the need for adequate artillery and air support, particularly close air support overhead as well as specialised ships able to manoeuver extremely close to land. LSTs. (Landing Ship Tanks)

Meteorological Requirements

Airborne troops required a full moon both as illumination for pilots, and to assist troops as they landed.

Warships required daylight hours to attack the coastal defences.

Landing craft were best scheduled to land shortly before dawn, midway between the low and high tides, with the tide coming in. Low tides early morning would improve the visibility to see the obstacles on the beaches.

First availability would be in June.

The RAF's meteorological team forecast that Sunday 4 or Monday 5 of June would present the most favourable weather conditions to launch the invasion. Eisenhower settled on the date of Monday 5 June as the date for operation Overlord.

M.F.M.4. records confirm that on 15 May 1944 Steve was still with 22 Beach Recovery Section but now transferred to the Royal Canadian Electrical Mechanical Engineers, the date seen as the official birth date of the RCEME. In my father's records it reads 'Transfer from RCOC to RCEME at 9th. I.B. W/Shops'

I quote again from Colonel Murray C. Johnston book CANADA'S CRAFTSMEN AT 50!

Preparation for invasion had three main aspects as far as the REME and the 100 RCEME who were seconded to REME for the invasion. The first was preparation of vehicles for the channel crossing and landing, including the waterproofing programme. The second was the repair and recovery plan when moving to embarkation points and finally loading which included route clearance, and final equipment especially battery tests and checks prior to loading. The Canadian units were served by Area A, Portsmouth, which had 19 marshalling camps with standing for 4,500 vehicles and 8 recovery posts.

From this opening sentence of Colonel Murray C. Johnston, on a personal note I learn that my father was one of the original 100 member of the Canadian Band of Brothers of the RCEME.

Towards the end of May, some two weeks prior to the proposed date of 5 June for D-Day, troops started to move out from base camps to their marshalling camps in preparation for embarkation. These transit camps were in fact sealed units and well-guarded so no one could get out when off duty. They were in fact totally cut off from the outside world. Here they were briefed as to their role and familiarised with the plans for their tasks in the invasion. Some were issued with maps while others worked from scale models of the area in which they would be landing. At the same time they were issued with French currency, leaving no doubt as to where they were going.

On the 31 May Allied troops started to board their ships and equipment was loaded. For the previous few days the weather had been glorious with bright sunny warm days and long light evenings. However, once the first troops had boarded their ships and set sail, the weather soon began to change and it became evident that a meteorological depression was rapidly settling in over the English Channel.

Therefore on the evening of 3 June, as the RAF meteorologists predicted that there would be a break in the weather for the 5 and 6 June, Eisenhower made the decision to postpone the invasion for some twenty-four hours. Those convoys that had sailed had to be recalled to port. With the weather changing for the worse, at least the Germans would not expect the Allies to launch an invasion in such inclement conditions.

Messages were sent via the BBC to SOE agents in France to warn the resistance that the invasion was imminent so they could start sabotaging the road and rail links in the Normandy area. These messages always broadcasted after the nine o'clock news. During the evening of the 4 June the meteorologists predicted improvements in the weather for the 6 June onwards. Very early the following morning at his staff meeting Eisenhower alone made the monumental decision:

'We go tomorrow 6 June'.

Chapter 21   Beach Organisation.

It became apparent that there was a need for beach organisation when planning for larger operations. This was outlined by the Chief of Combined Operations Admiral Lord Louis Mountbatten in 1942, obviously from lessons learnt from Dieppe in August of that year, and Beach Groups were formed in the UK and began to train in Scotland that year.

Insignia of these British Beach Groups & GHQ Troop Engineers.

The large organisation that was required, composed of specialists from all three of the armed services. The units selected for this work, apart from their own technical training, all received Combined Operations training and practised alongside each other in the months preceding the invasion.

These units were under the overall command of an army colonel supported by a Beach Sub Area Headquarters. Each Beach Sub Area organisation was composed of Royal Navy Beach Commando units, Army Beach Groups, an R.A.F. Beach Squadron and an R.A.F. Beach Balloon Squadron.

The Royal Navy Beach Commandos controlled the arrival and departure of vessels that were landing their cargoes on the beaches. In each R.N. Beach Commando were a Principal Beach Master (P.B.M.), an Assistant Principal Beach Master and two or three beach parties each consisting of a Beach- master, two Assistant Beach-masters and about 20 seamen. The largest RNC operation of the war was Neptune, the naval portion of Overlord. Nine parties F, J, L, P, Q, R, S, T and W (mostly Canadians) were assigned and trained for this, the largest amphibious operation of the war. RNCs were in the first wave to judge whether subsequent landing craft could land at the same points or divert elsewhere.

The RCEME plan for the assault, 3rd Canadian Division's RCEME worked as part of the overall 1st British Corps REME. In addition to its normal divisional repair and recovery responsibilities, RCEME was to contribute to the beach group organisation. During the first 48-hours, recovery was to be limited to recovery of vehicles: from landing craft: in the water at beach entry and beach exits.

Recovery on roads was to be limited to route clearance. During this same period repairs were to be limited to 'repair on the spot' with cannibalisation supplementing the limited repair parts available.

There was to be a Beach Recovery Section (BRS) as part of the Beach Group in each brigade sector, 23 BRS in 7th Brigade's and 22 BRS in 8th Brigade's.

Each BRS was comprised of 160 men made up from the four brigade workshops of the assault force. Each BRS was to establish a Drowned Vehicle Point (DVP) to which all vehicle casualties would be brought. This would become the centre of RCEME activity on the beaches here would be sited the cutting and welding equipment so essential to recovery functions.

The BRS would also assist in helping shove off landing craft stuck on the beaches, although repair of these craft was a naval responsibility. The first elements of the BRS, the BARVs and armoured tractors, were scheduled to land starting at H-plus-15 minutes right after the assault companies.

During my original research in August 2012, when tracing my father's war service in the UK, I visited the REME museum and also corresponded with their technical historian as to what the war time duties of REME personnel would have been then:

Beach recovery sections, both REME and RCEME were virtually identical and were equipped with Sherman Beach Armoured Recovery Vehicles and Armoured Caterpillar D8 tractors, as well as the usual wheeled recovery vehicles. Their role was to keep mine-free beach exits clear of stalled or damaged vehicles and to recover from the sea any drowned vehicles, particularly armour which might wreck incoming landing craft. The section formed part of a Beach Group. Each of these was based on an Infantry battalion but with added detachments, including RE (Royal Engineers) for mine clearance, REME (Royal Electrical Mechanical Engineers) for vehicle recovery and even RAF (Royal Air Force) personnel with small barrage balloons.

The infantry elements were to clear away remaining enemy after the assault forces had moved inland. Beach Group personnel wore steel helmets with a white ring around them above the rim. This identified them as men whose job was to stay in the beach area, so military police did not think they were holding back from the advance. Elements of each first wave beach recovery section came ashore within the first half hour of the landings, in order to fulfil their role. Some worked for several weeks continuously until relieved.

Each beach was fixed between certain points on the actual map and named, then as they were captured and cleared of the enemy and any mines etc. sub-divided further: similar to this chart:

Research from publications at the British National Archives Kew in Surrey.

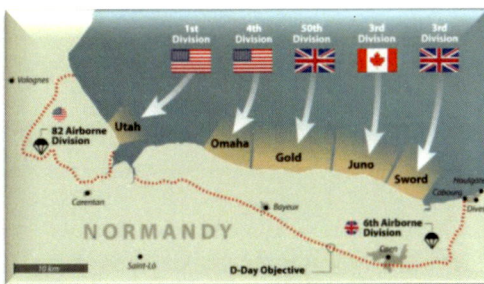

Each of the Army Beach Groups was based around an infantry battalion, responsible for an individual beach. The infantry both provided the bulk of the labour needed, as well as a significant combat capability, whether to seize key parts of the beach or to defend against counter-attacks. Attached to the battalion were specialists from the Royal Engineers to clear obstructions and prepare exit routes from the beach, the Royal Army Service Corps and Royal Army Ordnance Corps to handle supplies, beach recovery units from the Royal Electrical and Mechanical Engineers to clear damaged or drowned vehicles out of the way, Royal Army Medical Corps personnel to tend to casualties, Military Police to organise the traffic flow across the beach, and Pioneer Corps units to provide additional labour. As a phase was cleared and troops moved forward, this then allowed for the next wave of troops to move into these cleared positions, establishing the Drowned Vehicle Point (DVP) for any vehicle casualty's precise locations for the storage of petrol, ammunition, rations.

The opening gambit of operation Overlord was not, as one might think, by assault forces or Royal Navy beach commandos storming the beaches of Normandy, having just arrived by landing craft.   No that was not the case!

Sword Beach stretched some five miles to the small fishing port of Ouistreham that is also the estuary of both the River Orne and Caen Canal. One and a half miles inland from Ouistreham at the village of Bénouville is a road bridge across the canal, and along the same road, less than one and half miles apart to the west at the next village, Ranville, is a second bridge crossing the river Orne.

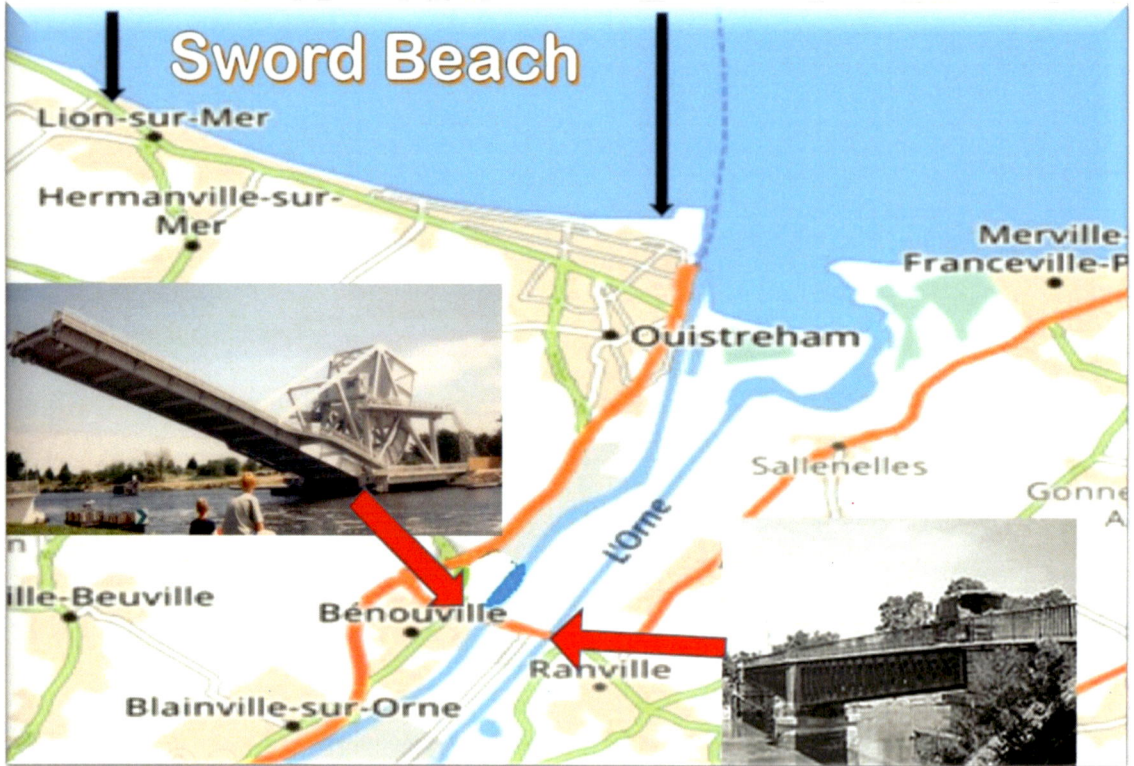

Intelligence reports suggested that both bridges were heavily defended by German forces and had been wired for demolition. When captured, the bridges had to be held on a 'hold until relieved' against any counter-attacks until the assault force was relieved by advancing troops from the British landing zone.

If the Germans retained control of the bridges these could be used to counter-attack the beach landings in Normandy. The bridges were equally vital to the success of the British airborne landings scheduled in this area, since if not captured, British airborne landings would be cut off from the rest of the Allied armies.

Operation Deadstick was the codename given to this British mission to 'Capture and Hold these two bridges'.

The commanding officer of the 6 Air-landing Brigades when asked to recommend the best troops for this action, nominated 'D' Company, 2nd (Airborne) Battalion
The Oxfordshire and Buckinghamshire Light Infantry.

A company of soldiers usually consists of between 80 to 250 men and is commanded by a captain or a major, depending on its overall size. These solders usually work together in smaller groups of between eight to ten men referred to as a platoon. For some tasks, the platoon can be divided into small groups of four to five men and referred to as a section. Sections work together, train together and live together.

Light infantry is a designation applied to certain types of foot soldiers, who often fought as scouts or raiders, soldiers who fight in a loose formation ahead of the main army. This regiment's history is traced back as far as July 1881. 'D' Company Oxfordshire and Buckinghamshire Light Infantry, were under the command of Major John Howard. He trained his troops incessantly day and night, utilizing bomb-damaged inner-city areas to practise, and prepare troops for street fighting using live ammunition when possible. After a few weeks training Major Howard became aware he would require more troops than just D Company for this mission. He selected two more platoons from 'B' Company Oxon & Bucks'. Changes were then made to the operational plan to accommodate six platoons.

It was not until early May, some five weeks prior to the operation that Major Howard was told of the exact details of his mission. His orders were to seize the bridges over the River Orne and Caen Canal at Bénouville and Ranville intact and hold them until relieved by the troops landing on Sword Beach.

To assist his battle plan thirty Royal Engineers from the 249 (Airborne) Field Company were assigned to his force, which now consisted of six infantry and one engineers platoon. (in military terms a 'reinforced company') Howard's battle plan was that three platoons would attack each bridge simultaneously. The Ox & Bucks troops would overcome the German guards, leaving the Sappers (nickname for royal engineers) to deal with any explosive charges found at

Royal Engineers

the bridges. The Royal Engineers history is traced back as far as 1716.

Outside the city of Exeter, in the south west of England, two bridges similar to their Normandy objectives had been identified crossing the River Exe. For a full week, by day and night, Major Howard's troops carried out practice exercises attacking and then defending these bridges simultaneously, day and night.

It was crucial to the mission that the elements of stealth and surprise were not compromised. Equally the force had to arrive at its precise location in tandem. With the targets being so close, there was the risk that noise at one bridge could rouse defenders at the other bridge. An airborne drop by parachute was ruled out, as troops could be blown off course or land in the river or canal or be spotted in the air due to aircraft engine noise.

Glider Pilots Regiment

A glider borne landing for attacking these two bridges was decided upon. Transport to Normandy was by Airspeed AS.51 Horsa gliders, piloted by 12 NCOs from 'C' Squadron, Glider Pilot Regiment from the Army Air Corps.

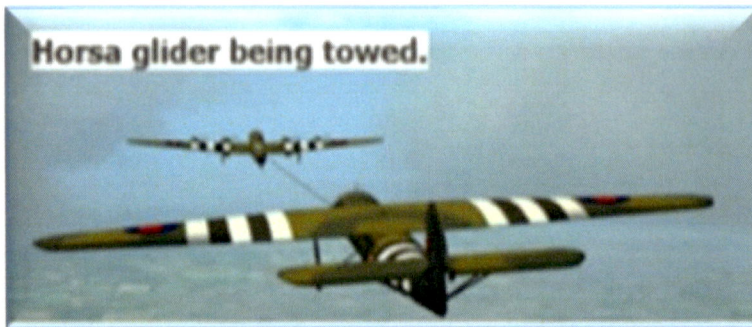

Horsa glider being towed.

Pilots trained using practice landings on small strips of land, marked out by tape. Horsa gliders were fitted with navigational instruments but the pilots practised flying using stopwatches to register accurate timings for the course changes when the gliders would be in free flight, about six miles away from their targets.

Flight crews also practised with dark glass fitted over their goggles, to get used to flying at night. By May 1944 they had carried out 54 training flights, flying in all weathers both day and night. At the end of May 1944, 'D' Company left the battalion camp at Bulford in Wiltshire for RAF Tarrant Rushton in Dorset. This base was then secured and Major Howard briefed everyone on the mission, distributing photographs of the bridges and unveiling a model of the area.

On the night of 5 June 1944, this force of 181 men boarded six Horsa gliders at RAF Tarrant Rushton, each carrying thirty members of the force, including one section of five Sappers in each glider. Just before the men boarded the gliders, code words were issued to wireless operators. 'Ham' indicated the canal bridge was captured and 'Jam' the river bridge. Around 10:30 pm that night the gliders left England, being towed by Halifax bombers.

After an approximate two hour flight they arrived at their cast off point for the free flight in to the target area, which was midway between Caen and the coast and about 6 miles from the bridges.

Five of the Ox and Bucks' gliders landed as close as 47 yards from their designated bridges the first at fifteen minutes past midnight with others arriving close behind - the first Allied troops to arrive in Normandy. The attackers poured out of their gliders, completely surprising the German defenders. After a brief fire fight, both bridges were captured, all within 10 minutes of them landing.

The Ox and Bucks lost just two men in this action. Lieutenant Denham Brotheridge was killed crossing the canal bridge in the first minutes of the assault and thus became the first member of the invading Allied armies to die as a result of enemy fire on D-Day. Lance-Corporal Fred Greenhalgh drowned in a nearby pond when his glider landed. One glider, assigned to the capture the Ranville river bridge, instead landed at the bridge over the River Dives, some seven miles off course. Most of the soldiers in that glider moved through German lines towards the village of Ranville where they eventually re-joined the British forces.

An all BRITISH affair was the opening battle of D-Day!
The bridge at Bénouville was renamed Pegasus Bridge in honour of that operation.

Air Chief Marshal Trafford Leigh-Mallory, of the Royal Air Force, praised the pilots involved saying the operation included the "most outstanding flying achievements of the war".

Neptune's day of days.

It was Bertram Ramsay, then a vice-admiral, who had masterminded the evacuation of some 338,226 British and allied troops from the beaches of Dunkirk, between 27 May and 4 June 1940. Now exactly four years later from the event that Winston Churchill hailed as a "miracle of deliverance", the Allies returned in strength to mainland Europe.

Operation Neptune, the codename given to the Royal Navy's role in the Normandy landings, was the largest naval operation during WWII. The Allies landed around 156,000 troops that day, in an armada of 6483 ships ranging from cargo carriers, destroyers, merchant vessels, mine sweepers, specialist craft, troop carriers and warships, all under the responsibility of the British Admiral Bertram Ramsay, commander of naval forces.

One of the first tasks for the 250 minesweepers preceding the main armada was clearing the seas and entrances to beaches of mines, with up to five levels or depths being cleared.

A few days prior to the invasion the shipping lanes had also been cleared and routes marked out using some 73 lighted buoys at various depths in given positions between England and France. Trinity House, an organization for the safety of shipping, and the wellbeing of seafarers, established the buoys and these were laid according to schedule, despite the poor weather conditions. Some of these marker buoys were sunk with delayed time switches attached to the metal cables mooring them to the sea bed. When activated, the switch would release the cables allowing the buoys to float to the surface on the day of the invasion. With the invasion being delayed these markers buoys surfaced some twenty four hours too early. Had they been spotted by any Luftwaffe reconnaissance missions, this could have given the game away.

Lighted buoys:

Therefore, the night before the armada sailed, a large number of Allied planes flew over northern France including 617 Squadron who using electronic devices when dropped out at sea, created a false picture on German radar of a large group of ships approaching the Pas de Calais. At the same time as the radar was jammed some seventeen hundred tons of bombs were being dropped on German coastal defenses.

In the next stages, the American and the British Parachute Battalion including the First Canadian parachute battalions, took off. The Canadians' DZ (Dropping Zone) was to the east of the river Orne on the left flank of the main British assault force. The success of the Allied eastern flank depended on the Canadians holding this ridge and preventing a German counter-attack from reaching the invasion forces on the beaches at Ouistreham. Because of bad weather the Germans were taken completely by surprise, with many of their commanders not being with their troops. In fact Erwin Rommel, now a Field Marshal, was away in Germany attending his wife's birthday. This showed that the armada was not expected.

HMS Belfast (Town-class light cruiser)

As the vast armada of ships started to approach the Normandy coast just prior to first light that Tuesday morning, infantry troops involved in the first wave attacks onto the beaches began to transfer to their landing crafts. The bombardment force comprised five battleships, two monitors, twenty cruisers and sixty-five destroyers. HMS Belfast was designated headquarters ship of Bombardment Force E and supported the landings by British and Canadian forces in the Gold and Juno Beach sectors. The invasion was to begin on Monday 5 June but bad weather forced a 24-hour delay. At 5:30 am on 6 June HMS Belfast opened fire on a German artillery battery at Ver-sur-Mer, suppressing the guns until the site was overrun by British infantry from the 7 Battalion, The Green Howards.

HMS Ramillies 1943

My next text is taken from the ships' log of HMS Ramillies:

Ramillies provided fire support for the Normandy Landings on 6 June 1944. Sword Beach, to the east, was her assigned area; she was given the primary task of silencing the Bernville battery. The ship began by opening fire on the 6" (152 mm) battery, knocking out four of the six guns in the first 80 minutes and keeping the attention of the rest, allowing landing craft to proceed unmolested. By evening she had accounted for the other two guns. During the course of the first day, she repelled an attack by two German destroyers which fired five torpedoes at her, all missing. Canadian destroyers HMCS Algonquin and HMCS Sioux took part in the bombardment force as did two Canadian Landing Ships Infantry (Medium) deliver troops HMCS Prince Henry and HMCS Prince David.

King George VI

Prime Minister Winston Churchill had announced his intention to go to sea with the fleet and witness this invasion on board HMS Belfast. This was opposed by both the Supreme Allied Commander General Eisenhower, and the First Sea Lord Sir Andrew Cunningham, but Churchill insisted on going. It was only when King George VI himself announced he would also attend. Then Winston aware of the Extreme danger to the King if he attended, Winston changed his mind about going, until a few days after D-Day.

Chapter 24

"A Sappers Tale"

My Recollections of D-Day.

By: L.G. Butt (Hon Capt.) Rtd
Royal Engineers.

This photo of Leonard Butt given to the author in October 2014, is taken from the Royal British Legions publication 'A D-Day Dozen' publication form that 60th anniversary in 2004 a select group of veterans who epitomise the gallantry and bravery of all those 'Anonymous Heroes' involved on D-Day 6 June 1944.

Decorations: worn in this photo: Top row left to right.

| 1939–1945 Star: | France & Germany star: | The War Medal: | Cadet Force Medal & Bar |

Normandy Veterans Association   **French Government**
                                          50th Anniversary of D-Day

Having discovered that Leonard landed on Juno Beach at the same time as my father, I was honoured when he agreed to write and let me publish his recollections of that monumental day, a living history a true account of D-Day and by someone who was there on that day.

That's me, the army cadet sergeant in March 1943 just two months before I joined the Royal Engineers. With less than a year's service, I found myself posted to 184 Field Company (Royal Engineers).At this time our unit was stationed on Netley Common on the outskirts of Southampton, a large tented camp we were sharing with the Canadian Nova Scotia Highlanders and a Canadian engineer company. They were a part of the 'Engineer' element for the 3rd Canadian division's beach group that would be at the forefront of our division's assault on the 'Atlantic Wall'.

My first experience of landing craft was on exercise 'Fabius III' in May that year when I was just eighteen. We sailed out of Southampton, landing the following morning on the beaches between East and West Wittering in Sussex.

During our absence the camp had been sealed off. From then on we would be confined to camp leaving it only on two further occasions, marching out with the other units of that division for inspection by VIP's. The first inspection was by Winston Churchill, General Smuts and Mr Mackenzie King, the second time by General Montgomery. After this we did not leave camp until we embarked for D-Day. Our remaining days were hectic, intensive a whirl wind of final preparations, briefings, and issuing of the specialist equipment, meaning more kit to carry.

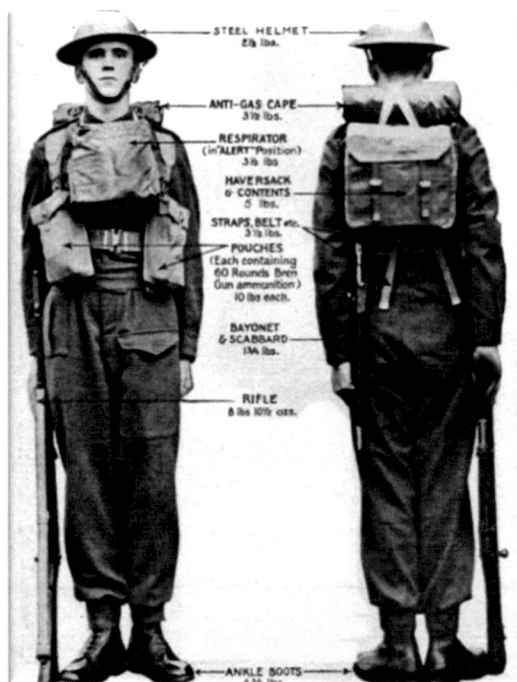

Pattern 38 webbing= Designed in 1938.

Amongst these specialist items were what was known as 'prepared charges' - explosive devices for demolition tasks. Each section would be required to carry one 25lbs 'prepared charge' and for some reason our section's satchel was issued to me.

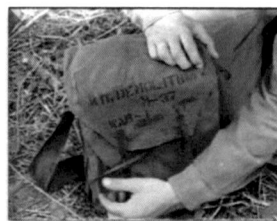

The Prepared charge.

We re-rehearsed packing and wearing our full kit, pattern 38 webbing which when packed weighed some 100lbs.

Platoon sergeant (Sgt) Brown, stopped to check my kit, patting the 'prepared charge' perched on top of my rucksack, and informed me that this was harmless until primed with the detonator and a fuse. He informed me even if hit by a bullet it was safe "unless it's a tracer bullet".

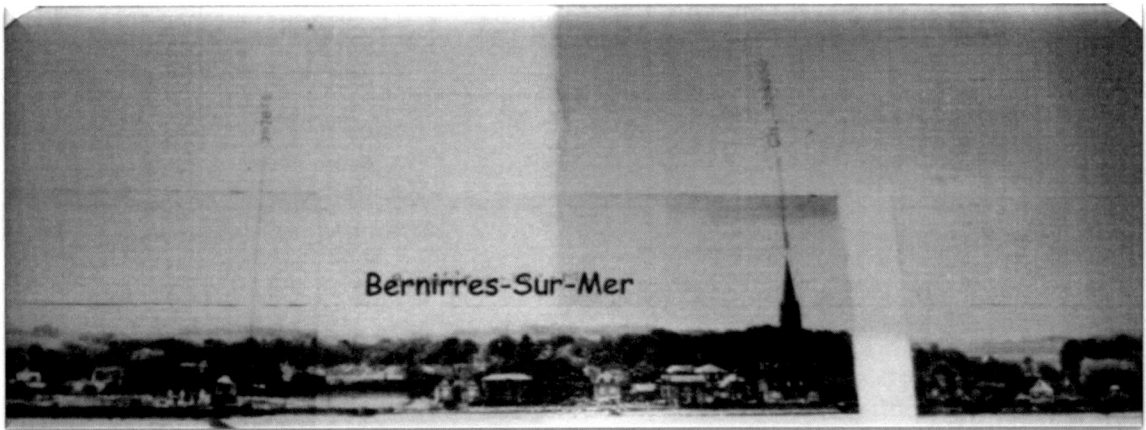

Bernirres-Sur-Mer

"Tracer bullets are built with a small pyrotechnic charge like white phosphorus in their base. Ignited by the burning powder, this composition burns very brightly, making the projectile visible to the naked eye. This enables the shooter to follow the projectile trajectory to make aiming corrections."

The maps and models used for our briefings over the next few days were in incredible detail these together with the aerial photographs, many taken at sea level, enabled us to form a very clear picture of our particular stretch of beach, including the beach obstacles and strong points that we had to deal with.
We discovered that we would be landing on Juno-Nan Beach, right in front of Bernirres-Sur-Mer, and that after disembarking we had to rendezvous by the sea wall. We then had to meet up with our Platoon Officer (Lt Phillips) and the reconnaissance Sgt who would be landing with the Assault Infantry the Queen's Own Rifles of Canada.
Thursday 1st.June 1944. Today the Company was addressed by the Commanding Officer, his main comments being:-
That he considered it a privilege that we were wearing the 3 Canadian's Divisional Flash and that we would be supporting the divisional assault on the Atlantic Wall.
He reminded us of the sacrifice made by the Canadians at Dieppe in August 1942 and how the lessons of that tragedy would be of benefit to us in the task ahead. He concluded by expressing his confidence that we would all do our utmost in supporting the division's assault.

Saturday 3rd.June 1944.

We awoke to discover the camp was now placed on instant readiness (ready to move out in one hour) and informed that as of now we were on 'Active Service'. (My army discharge book clearly states - Service NW Europe. 3.6.44.) We spent the day in an increasing state of tension. Each hour seemingly longer, until just before last light. Then into camp rolled a large convoy of TCV's (Troop Carrying Vehicles). Within a short time we had loaded up and were on our way into Southampton Docks. As we approached the dock area, convoys were approaching from all points of the compass, it was incredible. Yet such was the organisation and control that in a comparatively short time we had threaded our way to our allocated dock basin, where we unloaded

 and eventually embarked on our LCI –it was the same one as we had used on exercise 'Fabius III'. It was amazing that no one finished up in the water as we all had to scramble over several small craft before reaching our own vessel.

Library & Archives Canada, Photographer Gilbert Milne.

Landing Craft Infantry Large; are quite small vessels, some 180 feet long and with a very shallow draught of about five feet at the most. Our platoon accommodation was the forward hold, a steel box some twenty feet by twenty feet lined with tiers of steel bunk frames without bedding because of the fire risk. This was our transport for that Channel crossing arriving on board just before midday till the following morning. During exercise 'Fabius III' we had experienced balmy summer weather when we spent only one night on board. Even then under almost ideal weather we had found considerable discomfort cramped conditions with the overall pervading stench of diesel fumes, but our channel crossing would prove to be a far sterner test.

Sunday 4th June 1944. The morning found us still tied up in dock, but mid-morning we started out of the dock although with the enormous number of craft involved it was hours before we cleared the docks area, and started sailing up the Solent. Suddenly, to our amazement we were turning along with all the other craft, to spend the rest of the day returning to dock.

Rumours started as to why, until we noticed a rapid deterioration in the weather. It was nearly dark when we finally tied up once more. Then we were informed of a 24 hour postponement. Even in the relative shelter of the dock basin we were to spend a rough night on board.

Monday 5ʰ June 1944.

That morning we were given orders to leave our kit on board, and to disembark onto the quay to be fed and stretch our legs. We were still confined only to a dockside warehouse for this.   That afternoon the improvement in the weather meant we were ordered back on board. Later that afternoon we got underway again. Fortunately we were being allowed up on deck, from where we could see the Solent filling with ships and landing craft.

From the enormous dock complex of Southampton, to the River Hamble, every conceivable inlet was full of endless streams of vessels forming into convoys.

When underway that afternoon our Platoon Sgt opened his copy of the sealed orders and informed us in the morning we would be on the coast of Normandy. At last I knew for certain where we were going as a member of the third expeditionary force to sail to the continent in the past thirty years. We were ordered off deck I took a final look at home, and went below. As we cleared the eastern tip of the Isle of Wight, heading for the assembly area some ten miles out, we became fully aware just how rough the sea still was in the aftermath of the storm that delayed D-Day.

Our craft was buffeted by waves five to six feet high and with most men soon reduced to sea sickness, the stench was overpowering. After midnight we could hear the drone of aeroplane engines above the noise of the waves pounding on the side of the ship, getting louder as they approached. By the time they passed overhead the noise was deafening. This was the sixth airborne armada on its way to its DZ (Dropping Zone) over Normandy.

Tuesday 6th June D-day 1944.

At dawn we sorted ourselves out, and received orders to get our kit on and into positions for landing. I was lucky to be the second in the queue and on to the starboard gangplank. So I was up on deck sheltering behind the forward hatch, able to see over both sides of the craft. We were about ten miles out and started our drive towards the beach. As we did, we passed close to the Allied warships HMS Ramillies, the Lord Roberts, Warspite and others. Then we passed HMS Belfast and Diadem and finally through the destroyer and gunboat screen. Everyone seemed to be shooting and the noise was deafening. With about a mile to go we were warned to prepare for beaching and to hitch up our webbing.

Photo a137013 by kind permission of Library and Archives Canada (Photographer: Gilbert Milne)

With a hard jolt we beached and I followed Sgt Brown down the gangplank, plunging off into chest high water as we waded ashore.

To my amazement there in front of me was the sea wall at Bernieres, we had landed exactly as planned during our briefings. It was 08:00 hrs which meant we had arrived late by thirty minutes. As previously ordered, we quickly gathered by the sea wall and began to reconnoitre the situation.

We were not waiting long. Sgt Brown started to issue orders and I found myself detailed with my section to clear mines from the dunes on top of the sea wall.

I had been trained to use the Polish mine detector that we had been issued with. It had a ten foot sweeping arm when extended and a total weight of some fifteen pounds. The rest of the platoons were set to work on the mass of obstacles along the foreshore, many of these being mined. Armoured bulldozers were already at work and a flail tank had cleared two exits off the beach and an armoured ramp had been laid enabling vehicles to get off the beach. The landings at Bernieres had been further delayed by bad weather. Starting some thirty minutes late caused a considerable handicap for beach clearance, with the tide now coming back in covered many obstacles before they could finally be cleared. It would take until early afternoon before the beach could be reasonably cleared. Nevertheless sufficient progress was made to enable the follow up brigade and artillery units to start landing some two hours after H-Hour.

We started our clearance task and I found myself operating our mine detector. Using this I started my first sweep then stopped immediately -there at my feet was my first mine. Indicating this to my number two whose job it was to mark the mines when found, when he came forward to place a marker, he stopped then looked at me. I looked back at him and then at the mine. It was a type we had not seen nor been instructed about and turned out to be a Belgian mine. This was a problem that was to occur quite often. We realised that during our all too brief training in the UK many of us had only seen and handled British, German and Italian mines, a problem that was overcome but only at the expense of unnecessary casualties.

The German Schu-mine 42 (Shoe-mine), was an anti-personnel mine. This was a simple wooden box with a hinged lid containing a seven ounce block of cast TNT and a detonator. If you pressed down on the lid, like stepping on it, it released the striker which triggered the detonator and would blow your leg off. They were cheap to produce and deployed in large numbers in Normandy.
The wooden box made it more difficult to detect with a metal / mine detector.

On landing few of us paid much attention to the conditions on the beach, being intent on reaching our RV (rendezvous point) by the sea wall; but now as we got to work, we began to realise just how fortunate we had been. There were a considerable number of casualties around. As well as the wrecked tanks and landing craft at intervals along the beach we discovered that all of our reconnaissance section were among the casualties.

Lt. Phillips our platoon officer, was shot by a sniper, the reconnaissance sergeant and two of the sappers also dead. By the end of the day some twenty percent of our platoon were among the casualties. About two hours after H-Hour, the follow up brigade started landing. We were quite surprised when from a fresh wave of LCIs, The Nova Scotia Highlanders, came streaming ashore carrying folding bicycles. At that time, Jerry was still barely a mile up the road; one of our lads called out that they would not be able to claim mileage allowance for using bicycles. Nevertheless the Nova Scotia Highlanders would have the last laugh by making the deepest infantry penetration inland on D-Day.

Early that evening an alarm was raised that a German counter-attack had broken through to the beach between us and Sword beach. We stood to with weapons loaded and ready. We waited events with some apprehension. Time ticked by with tension mounting. Suddenly from across the Channel came the sound of many aircraft. The noise grew louder and louder rising, above the current sounds around us. Then what a sight to behold -the 6 Air Landing Brigade coming in to reinforce the 6th Airborne Division, some five hundred tugs all with gliders in tow.

Spontaneous cheering echoed around the beach as the gliders were detached and swooped into land. The sky looked to be filled with anti-aircraft fire, very few aircraft seemed to be hit. With the arrival of the airborne reinforcement all tension had vanished. The general feeling was that we were here to stay. Just before last light, some four or five German bombers appeared overhead, dropping bombs at random, but they all got shot down. As a young green sapper, I hoped I had played my part on that Day.

I had been lucky seeing both the sunrise and set; for others did not.

Chapter 25 **Time Line on Juno.**

Taken by the RAF Photographic Reconnaissance Unit on D-Day at H-Hour.

My next text taken from Colonel Murray C. Johnston's book, CANADA'S CRAFTSMEN.

The Assault

'**WIND** - west, force 15 knots; **SEA** - moderate, waves 3 to 4 feet; **SKY** - fair to cloudy with cloud increasing.' These few words summarised the weather for the assault beaches at dawn on 6 June 1944. Because H-hour was ten minutes later than originally planned and the wind was so strong it drove the tide in-shore half an hour ahead of its time, assault craft landed amongst beach obstacles instead of in front of them. This along with the enemy mines took a heavy toll on landing craft until the obstacles were cleared at next ebb tide. (End of quote)

05:35	German shore batteries open fire: Allied naval forces, now massed along the entire Normandy coast, begin their bombardment.
06:30	Assault on to the beaches starts. 3rd Canadian Divisions landings made difficult by strong current. This delay allows Germans to mount strong defence objective. Assault troops advance inland and join troops from British beaches. Infantry battalions have five RCEME personnel on strength – two vehicle mechanics for the universal carriers and three armourers. The Part 2 Orders of the assaulting battalions show that most if not all of the battalions RCEME people landed with the first waves. **All Beach Recovery Sections in place.**
07:00	German radio broadcast first report of landing.
07:58	6 Canadian armoured regiment (1Hussars) Regimental history reports: In support of the 7th Canadian Infantry Brigade of the 3rd Canadian Division assaulted and overpowered the German defences between Courseulles-sur-Mer and Bernières-sur-Mer.

07:58	7th Brigade Sector. Because there was a further twenty-minute delay caused by the weather it had been decided not to launch the 1 Hussar's tanks. Then the decision was reversed and two squadrons were launched. 'B' Squadron was launched 4,000 yards from shore and landed 15 out of 19 tanks on the proper beach at 0758 hours followed in 15 minutes by the infantry. The order to launch 'A' Squadron came later at 1,500 yards from shore. However, the squadrons' formation was disrupted by fire and the rough and unruly weather. In the end, some tanks were not launched but were landed directly on the beach after the infantry had landed
08:30	48 Commando lands at St Aubin-sur-Mer, Juno Nan beach and head east.

Beach Clearance difficult due to high tides and rough seas.

09:00	54 LAD RCEME supporting the 1st Hussars landed at 0900 hours, thus becoming the first LAD RCEME crew to land in Normandy. They immediately went to work on the regiment's tanks that had bogged down or been put out of commission. This small group examined all disabled tanks, repaired or recovered what they could and then moved inland to their assembly area.
09:35	Canadian 8th Brigade liberate Bernières-sur-Mer Juno Beach Nan sector.
11:12	After a fierce fire fight 7th brigade secure the Juno exit at Courseulles-Sur-Mer but congestion occurred as Canadian 9th brigade arrive.
11:20	Canadians capture Tailleville, Banville and St. Croix.
13:35	German 352 Division wrongly advise HQ Berlin that the Allied assault repulsed. This message was not corrected until 18:00 same day.
14:15	All 3 Canadian Division on shore, rapid advances start, troops link up with Gold beach.
18:00	3 Canadian Division North Nova Scotia Highlanders reach three miles inland. 50 Division at Creully, After the village is captured, 'C' Squadron 1 Hussars tanks press on, with 2nd Troop reaching the regiment's objective of the Caen-Bayeux Highway, some 10 miles inland becoming the only Allied unit to reach its D-Day objective. Canadian Scottish link with 50 Division at Creully.

The Canadians landed 21,400 troops on Juno that day and suffered 1,200 casualties a casualty ratio of 1 out of 18.

The Beach recovery sections' role was to keep mine-free beach exits clear of stalled or damaged vehicles, and to recover from the sea any drowned vehicles, particularly armour which might wreck incoming landing craft. They used BARVs and Armoured Caterpillar D8 tractors for this work.

This text taken from Colonel Murray C. Johnston book CANADA'S CRAFTSMEN.

The reserve unit of 8th Brigade, le Régiment de la Chaudière, started to land at Bernières-sur-Mer at 0830 hours. Craftsman C.A. MacDonald, one of the unit's armourers, drove a 15-cwt truck loaded with 6-pounder anti-tank gun ammunition. He recalled: 'I had to wait about 50 feet offshore for a few minutes while a bulldozer knocked a hole in the sea wall so that I could get ashore.' **(End quote)**

My father was seconded to 22 BRS REME. This unit first appeared in the official War Office files at National Archives Kew referenced WO 166/13636 dated November 1943. We now know why RCEME craftsman were training for many months before.

M.F.M.4. confirms that on 15 May 44 B-52942 Steve Alexson was seconded to 22 BRS also on active service NW Europe as and from 3 June and landed with the assault troops on D-Day.

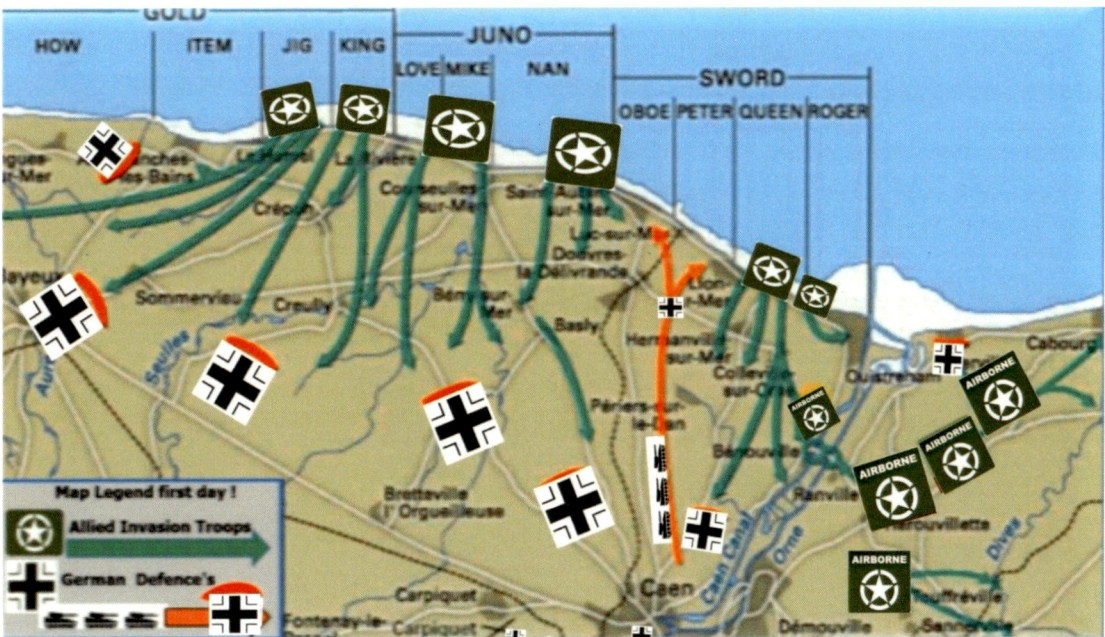

Allied positions for Gold Juno & Sword establish on D-day 6th. June 1944.

After thirty-seven days working on Juno he was wounded on 13 July 44 then evacuated to the British Base Field Hospital at Bayeux Normandy.M.F.M.4. Confirms that on 17 July 44 he was evacuated back to 22nd Canadian General Hospital in England listed as X3.

X List Classifications:

X 1=	Prisoners of War. (Verified)	**X 7=**	All ranks seconded from the Canadian Army to other Allied Forces in the theatre of war.
X 2=	All ranks under sentence of detention, imprisonment or penal servitude.	**X 8=**	All non-effective held at Base Reinforcement Units whose return to the UK has been authorised.
X 3=	All ranks evacuated on medical grounds behind Regimental Aid Posts.	**X 9=**	All personnel held at base reinforcement Units for one reason or another are not available as reinforcement and whose disposition is still to be decided.
X 4=	Un-posted reinforcements in the theatre of war belonging to the unit or corps.	**X 10=**	All reinforcement personnel attached away from reinforcement units under appropriate authority.
X 5=	All ranks on courses of 21 days or over in the theatre of war.	**X 11=**	All Red Cross and Auxiliary Services Personnel.
X 6=	All ranks posted as missing.	**X 12=**	At depot awaiting discharge.

On my last visit to the British National Archives at Kew on Thursday, 24 July 2014, I was to discover the following circumstantial evidence in the official records:

From file WO 177/955 with file WO 222/917 an entry from 13 July 44, 2nd Field Hospital REME at BAYEUX: '6 British casualties admitted + 2 German wounded POW's.'
From the same files the entry of 17 July '44 'Two discharged today, one requisitioned for Air Transport to the UK, the other sea evacuation'.

To close with now just a little more déjà vu : some Canadian troops acted as interpreters during the interrogation of some of the German POWs who in fact were Russian and spoke only Ukrainian.

I dedicate this work to all of the Anonymous Heroes, the Craftsmen and Sappers, those "Anonymous Heroes" who played their part leading up to and after D-Day working on all of the beaches until the Germans surrendered unconditionally on the 7th May 1945.

By documenting the research I discovered from those Official Records and the War Diaries stored at the National Archives at Kew, the Regimental Diaries stored at various regimental depots in England as well as research supplied by the Canadian Veteran's Association, this work can now serve as a reminder of just how much Operation Overlord achieved just four years after the deliverance of Dunkirk in June 1940.

British Beach Group Organization

Britain formed these units from all three services – the Royal Navy (Commandos), British Army and the Royal Air Force, with the Army component comprising Infantry, Engineers, Ordnance, Royal Electrical and Mechanical Engineers, Medical and Service Corps.

Shoulder insignia worn by beach group personnel.

The complement of a Beach group up to 3000 men.

Reinforcements

IT was imperative to keep beaches open to allow reinforcements and supplies to flow freely inland in support of advancing troops. Reinforcements must arrive quicker than the Germans could reinforce to make any counter attacks.

It was imperative to build up supplies of stores and equipment and move these forward away from the beaches. My research proved that for some weeks after D-day the beaches were still under attack. Records show on the 9 July 44 (that is 32 days after D-Day) an ammunitions ship was hit by German action and blown up whilst being unloaded.

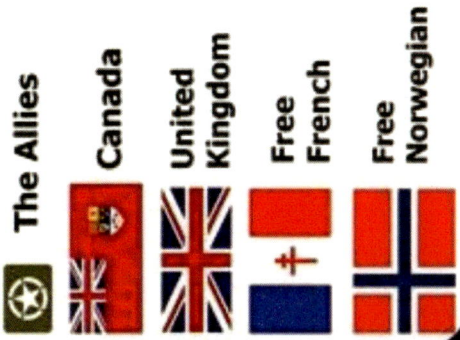

The Allies

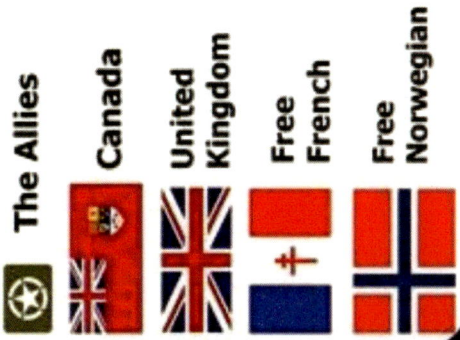	**Canada**
	United Kingdom
	Free French
	Free Norwegian

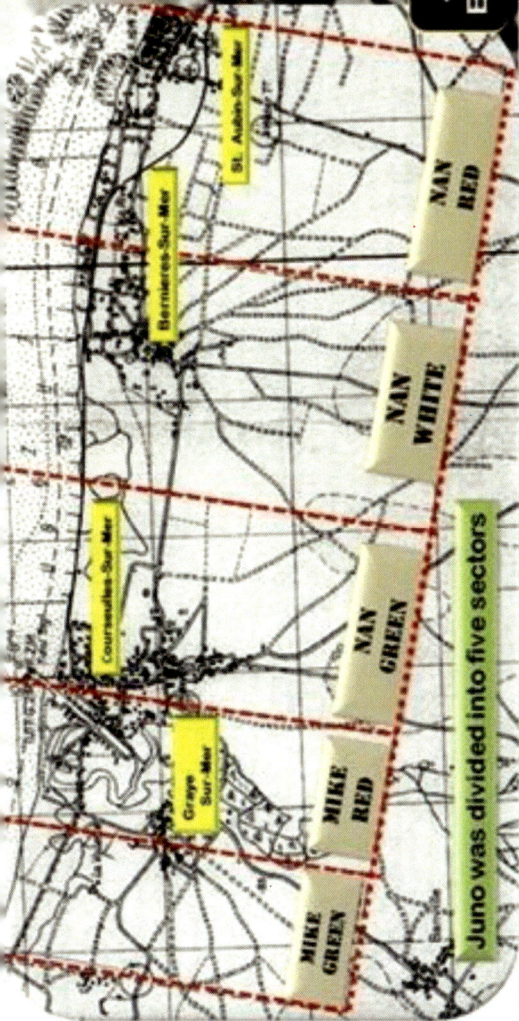

JUNO BEACH

Love sector:

This sector of Juno west of Corseulles-sur-mer, was used for off-loading equipment.

Juno was divided into five sectors

Mike sector: 23 Beach Recovery Section

1st Battalion, The Royal Winnipeg Rifles
1st Battalion, The Canadian Scottish Regiment (Victoria)
6 Armoured Regiment 1 Hussars 🚂 DD's
1st Battalion, The Cameron Highlanders of Ottawa (Machine Gun)
7 Canadian Infantry Brigade Ground Defence Platoon Lorne Scots.

Nan sector: 22 Beach Recovery Section

1st Battalion, The Regina Rifle Regiment
1st Battalion, The Queen's Own Rifles of Canada (Toronto)
1st Battalion, The North Shore (New Brunswick) Regiment
1st Battalion, Le Régiment de la Chaudière (Lévis, Quebec) 🚂 DD's
10 Armoured Regiment The Fort Garry Horse 🚂 DD's
8 Canadian Infantry Brigade Ground Defence Platoon Lorne Scots.

Follow-up forces landed in Nan Sector:

1st Battalion, The Highland Light Infantry of Canada (Galt, Ontario)
1st Battalion, The Stormont, Dundas and Glengarry Highlanders (Cornwall, Ontario)
1st Battalion, The North Nova Scotia Highlanders
27 Armoured Regiment The Sherbrooke Fusiliers Regiment (Quebec) 🚂 🚂 🚂
1st Battalion, The Cameron Highlanders of Ottawa (Machine Gun)
9 Canadian Infantry Brigade Ground Defence Platoon Lorne Scots

Support units integrated with troops in both Mike Sector and Nan Sector

Royal Regiment of Canadian Artillery (12, 13, 14, and 19 Field Regiments)
Observer elements only, 7 Reconnaissance Regiment 17 Duke of York's Royal Canadian Hussars (Montreal)
3 Anti-Tank Regiment   4 Light Anti-Aircraft Regiment   No. 3 Defence and Employment Platoon Lorne Scots
Corps of Royal Canadian Engineers   5 Canadian Field Company   6 Canadian Field Company
16 Canadian Field Company   18 Canadian Field Company
Royal Canadian Army Medical Corps   Royal Canadian Corps of Signals   Royal Canadian Army Service Corps   Royal Canadian Ordnance Corps

7 Beach Group in Mike sector 8 Irish Battalion King's Regiment   8 Beach Group in Nan sector 5 Battalion Royal Berkshire Regiment

British beach support forces:
HQ. 4 Special Service Brigade
48 Royal Marine Commando
AVRE from **79 Armoured Division**
B Squadron, 22 Dragoons Royal Armoured Corps Sherman Crab Mine flail
Royal Engineers
HQ 5 Assault Regiment
26 Assault Squadron
80 Assault Squadron
71 Field Company
72 Field Company
85 Field Company
184 Field Company
240 Field Company
262 Field Company
3 and 4 Batteries, 2 Royal Marine Armoured Support Regiment
Royal Artillery: Elements of 114 Light Anti-Aircraft Regiment & Elements of 93 Light Anti-Aircraft Regiment, : In reserve was No.4 Beach Group

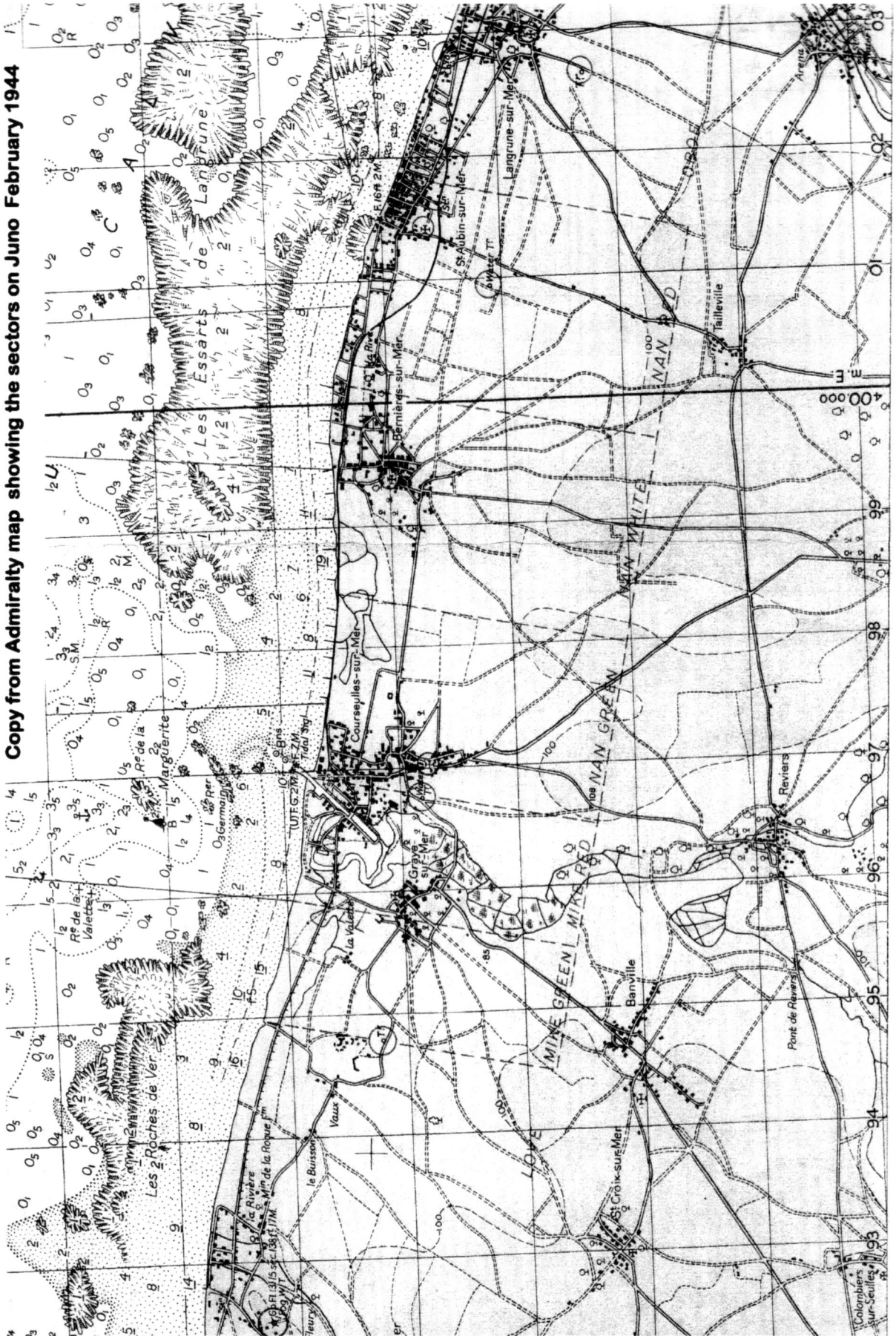

Glossary of Abbreviations - German Military references - Military Terminology.

A

Abwehr	German Military Intelligence
Afrikakorps	German Expeditionary force in North Africa
AFV	Armoured Fighting Vehicles
Allies of WW II	The anti- Nazi German coalition at the start of the war (1 September 1939) consisted of France, Poland and Great Britain, soon to be joined by the British Commonwealth (Canada, Australia, New Zealand, Newfoundland and South Africa.) Brazil was the only independent South American country to send ground troops to fight in the Second World War. On July 16, 1944 the first five thousand BEF soldiers arrived in Italy.
AQMS	Artificer Quarter Master Sergeant
Axis Forces	Nazi Germany, Italy and Japan

B

BDST	British Double Summer Time
BEF	British Expeditionary Force
Blitzkrieg	German expression for lightning war
BP	Bletchley Park
BRS	Beach Recovery Section
BSAC	Birmingham Small Arms Company

C

1 CBW	First Canadian Base Workshop
CIU	Central Interpretation Unit
COSSAC	Chief of Staff Supreme Allied Commander

D

DZ	Dropping Zone

F

Fallschirmjäger	Parachute Division
FF	Free French troops:
FUSAG	First United States Army Group

G

GMC	General Motor Corporation
GS 4 x 4 lorry	General service four wheel drive lorry.
Gestapo	Official secret police of Nazi Germany

K

Kriegsmarine	German Navy

L

LAD	Light Aid Detachment
LCI	Landing Craft Infantry
LST	Landing Ship Tanks
Luftwaffe	German air force

M

M.F.M.4.	Canadian military service and casualty records
MI5	British Security Service
Militia	Military force made up of civilians
MOD	Ministry of Defence

N	
Nazi Germany	Common name for Germany during the period from 1933 to 1945, when its government was controlled by Adolf Hitler and his National Socialist German Workers' Party (NSDAP), commonly known as the Nazi Party. Under Hitler's rule, Germany was racism, especially anti-Semitism, was a central feature of the regime that transformed into a fascist totalitarian state.
NCO	None Commissioned Officer

O	
OSS	America Office of Strategic Services

P	
PBM	Principal Beach-master
PBY Catalina	Amphibious aircraft / Sea Plane
Panzer division	German Tank division
P O & L	Petrol Oil & Lubricant
Pluto	Pipe-Lines Under The Ocean

R	
RAF	Royal Air Force
RCEME	Royal Canadian Electrical Mechanical Engineers
RCOC	Royal Canadian Ordnance Corps
REME	Royal Electrical Mechanical Engineers
RN	Royal Navy
RNC	Royal Navy Commando

S	
SIS	British Secret Intelligence Service
SOE	Special Operations Executive

T	
TCV's	Troop Carrying Vehicles

U	
U-Boat	German Sub-Marine
USAF	United States Army Air force
Ultra	Information obtained Via Bletchley Park

V	
VC	Victoria Cross
VRD	Vehicle Receiving Depot.

W	
WAAF	The Women's Auxiliary Air Force
Wehrmacht	German Army
WO	Warrant Officer Artificer Quarter Master Sergeant = WO
WRNS	Women's Royal Naval Service
WWI	World War One
WWII	World War Two

X	
X-List	A classification of serving personnel status